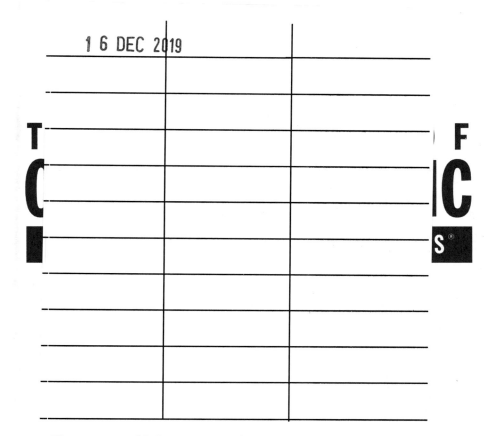

1 6 DEC 2019

T
C
I

F
C
S ®

Please return this book on or before the date shown above. To renew go to www.essex.gov.uk/libraries, ring 0845 603 7628 or go to any Essex library.

Essex County Council

THE HISTORY OF CLASSICAL MUSIC
FOR BEGINNERS

WRITTEN BY
R. Ryan Endris

ILLUSTRATED BY
JOE LEE

FOR BEGINNERS®

Published by For Beginners LLC
155 Main Street, Suite 211
Danbury, CT 06810 USA
www.forbeginnersbooks.com

Text: ©2014 R. Ryan Endris
Illustrations: ©2014 Joe Lee

Design and composition by Tim E. Ogline / Ogline Design

A For Beginners˙ Documentary Comic Book

Cataloging-in-Publication information is available from the Library of Congress.

ISBN # 978-1-939994-27-1 Trade

Manufactured in the United States of America

For Beginners˙ and Beginners Documentary Comic Books˙
are published by For Beginners LLC.

First Edition

10 9 8 7 6 5 4 3 2 1

Contents

Preface

The History of Classical Music For Beginners was the brain-child of illustrator Joe Lee and me. My dear friend Joe and I met while I was studying and working in Bloomington, Ind. Before I moved to New York to teach on the music faculty at Colgate University, we began talking about a niche that needed filling. Joe has written and illustrated many books in the For Beginners series, and we both felt that the series needed a book about the history of the music we commonly call "classical music." I am extremely grateful to Joe for agreeing to team up with me in the making of this book.

The History of Classical Music For Beginners provides the necessary scholarly muscle to entice and inform the reader, yet it does not require an understanding of music theory or force the reader to wade through hundreds of pages of jargon and details. Anyone can pick up this book and instantly start learning about—and understanding—classical music. Music theory, the study of *how* music is written and the fundamental elements of music, is excluded from the discussion of music to the greatest extent possible, so that one can read and understand without prior musical knowledge. The use of jargon and terminology has been kept to a minimum; in instances where it is necessary, a straightforward explanation is provided both in the prose and in the glossary. The words are both italicized and bolded the first time they are presented to draw the reader's attention to them.

Covering fifteen hundred years of music history is no easy task. Doing so in the span of a couple hundred pages is even more difficult, necessitating the exclusion of some musical styles and composers. You will notice that even some notable composers (like Tchaikovsky) are absent from this book. The aim of this book is to cover those musical styles and composers who exerted the *greatest* influence in the history of classical music to give the reader the greatest overall understanding of classical music possible. For example, opera is a genre of classical music that has an entire history of its own, and thus is discussed in only one chapter as part of a larger discussion of stylistic developments. Those wanting to know more about opera in music history should read *The History of Opera For Beginners* by Ron David. In fact, I encourage you to read and discover more about any composer, music, or topic that especially piques your interest while reading this book!

— **R. Ryan Endris**
Hamilton, New York
March 2014

I

MUSIC OF THE
ANCIENT AND
MEDIEVAL WORLDS

Chapter 1

ANCIENT MUSIC
AND PHILOSOPHY

Many people think of the music of Palestrina, Bach, and Mozart as "old music," but the earliest known instruments date to before 36,000 B.C.E.! Today, society considers music as part of the arts, but the ancient Greeks viewed it as part of the sciences. In fact, music was considered as important of a subject as astronomy, rhetoric, and math, and it was often taught alongside those other subjects. The music of ancient Greece (ca. 500 B.C.E.) focused on the role of numbers and mathematics in music. For example, Pythagoras used simple mathematical ratios to define consonances in music of the perfect fourth (4:3), perfect fifth (3:2), and perfect octave (2:1), which are still considered and labeled perfect sonorities to this day. He discovered that when a string is divided into segments with ratios of those lengths, those are the sonorities that sound.

Pythagoras pro-
posed the theory of *musica
universalis*, or "music of the spheres," the theory that the planets, sun,
and moon all produce a sound or hum based on their orbits. The sounds
produced by the celestial bodies, while inaudible and imperceptible to
humans, indeed had an effect on the quality of life of the inhabitants
of the earth. In his book *The Republic*, Plato also proposed that the
study of music and astronomy were linked by mathematics and numeri-
cal proportions. Because numbers inherently governed musical rhythms
and sound, music was reflective of the unification of parts in an orderly
whole. In this way, music was a prime example of an order that could be
sought in other areas, such as philosophy or the structure of societies.

Early Greek writers believed that music could affect one's ethos, or
way of being and behaving. Aristotle wrote of this in his *Politics*: music of a particular emotion or feeling was capable of evoking that same
emotion or feeling in the listener. This idea is rooted in the Pythagorean
view of music as a system of pitch and rhythm associated with the same

mathematical laws that governed the visible and invisible world. They believed that the human soul was comprised of parts kept in harmony by these orderly systems, and thus music had the potential of infiltrating the human soul. Both Plato and Aristotle held the idea that music was on equal footing with gymnastics in one's education. Gymnastics were intended to provide discipline for the body, while music was to provide discipline for the mind.

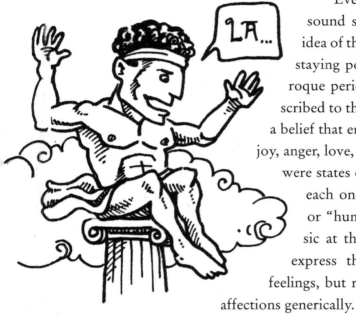

Even though this might sound silly to one at first, this idea of the ethos of music has had staying power. Even into the Baroque period, composers still prescribed to the *doctrine of affections*, a belief that emotions such as sadness, joy, anger, love, wonder, and excitement were states of being in the soul, and each one was caused by spirits, or "humors," in the body. Music at this time did not seek to express the composer's personal feelings, but rather sought to portray affections generically.

George Friedrich Handel's oratorio captures both the Ancient Greek and contemporary views on music and affections. The choral-orchestral work describes a banquet held by Alexander the Great and his mistress Thaïs in the captured Persian city of Persepolis. Throughout the banquet, the musician Timotheus sings and plays his lyre, effecting various moods and behavior in Alexander and his guests. In the end, Timotheus finally incites Alexander to burn the city to the ground in retribution for the Greek soldiers who died in battle. (You'll learn more about Handel and oratorio in Chapter 15).

Now back to the ancient Greeks! Very little ancient Greek music actually survives; only a handful of pieces or fragments of music from ancient Greece exist today, and those are primarily dated from 500 B.C.E. to 400 C.E. One reason for this is that there simply did not exist a true method for notating music; rather, musicians relied on their knowledge of musical conventions to perform and relay music. Those scraps of music that we do know of are simply letters and signs placed above the text, looking nothing like what we view today as musical notation. Two important pieces of ancient Greek music that do remain are the Seikilos Epitaph (music and text inscribed in a stone slab) and a choral ode called *Orestes* by the Euripides. Euripides' *Orestes,* as you might imagine, is the typical Greek tragedy, in which the women of Argos seek the mercy of the Gods for Orestes, who has killed his mother for committing adultery against his father, Agamemnon.

If it seems that we know very little about music in ancient Greece, then we know practically nothing about the music of ancient Rome. Primary sources include images of instruments and written documents about music, but there are no actual pieces of music that survive from the period of ancient Rome. We do know that the Romans adopted much of their musical culture from the ancient Greeks. Music played a large role in public ceremonies, and in the first and second centuries C.E., many aspects of Greek art and culture made their way over to Rome. Many of the emperors were patrons of music, including Nero, who fancied himself a musician and even competed in musical contests! Sadly, there does not seem to be any evidence of Roman music having any lasting effect on the development of Western Music.

In spite of how little music the ancient world left behind for us, we do know a number of important facts about that music. We know that the music focused primarily on melody, with a particular emphasis on the connection to rhythm and text. We know that there was no organized system of notating music, and thus musicians memorized music or relied on the knowledge of conventions. And we know that music was intimately connected with the sciences, resulting in an acoustical theory by Pythagoras and philosophers who viewed music as an intrinsic part of the universe with the power to affect the natural world and human behavior. As mentioned earlier, the ancient Greeks had a lasting influence on the development of Western music, and we'll continue to explore those ideas as we journey through the history of classical music.

Chapter 2

MUSIC IN THE EARLY CHURCH

he history of the Christian church, the principal social institution in the Middle Ages, is inextricably linked with the history of music in medieval Europe. Many of the characteristics of Western art music developed out of the needs of the church, from the development of musical notation to the advent of polyphony. With the church as a major player in the development of Western music in the Middle Ages, it comes as no surprise that church music from that era was the best preserved for posterity.

Given that Christianity began as an offshoot of Judaism, many of the Christian musical traditions came from the Jewish musical traditions. One prime example of this is the singing of psalms, sacred songs or hymns, found in the Hebrew Book of Psalms. Likewise, as *cantillation* (chanting of sacred texts) was and is commonplace in the Jewish synagogue, it also found a home in Christianity through various forms of chant, the most well-known being Gregorian chant. Just as theological (and political) divisions resulted in varying forms of rites, liturgies, and church calendars, divisions in the church resulted in a number of chant dialects, including Gregorian, Byzantine, Ambrosian, and Old Roman chant.

The Byzantine Church, the predecessor to modern-day Orthodox churches, held services that included Scriptural readings that were chanted. The melodies of the Scriptural chants reflected the text's phrasing and were developed based on formulas, while those chants of hymns and psalms were fully developed melodies. The hymn chants, by far the most pervasive and permanent characteristic of the Byzantine Church, were notated in books as early as the tenth century, and many of the chants are still sung in Greek Orthodox services today.

In the Western Church, the most important religious and musical center outside of Rome was the city of Milan. The songs and chants that developed in this northern Italian city became known as Ambrosian chant, named after St. Ambrose, the bishop of Milan between the years 374 and 397. Although there have been movements to suppress them, Ambrosian liturgy and chant still survive in Milan to this day, and they do share common characteristics with those of Rome.

Gregorian chant is the codified liturgy and musical repertory that developed under the Roman leadership with assistance from Frankish kings. The papal choir called the Schola Cantorum (School of Singers) most likely had an influence in the standardization of the chants in the late seventh century, as this choir performed whenever the pope presided in observances. The Frankish kingdom also helped solidify these chant melodies through an order that the Roman liturgy and music be performed throughout that kingdom. The Franks, of course, contributed to this body of liturgical music through their own additions and alterations.

This Frankish-Roman collaboration led to the standardization of chant that is attributed to Pope Gregory I (r. 590-604), who was revered as the founder of the Western church. As noted previously, the Schola Cantorum most likely cemented Gregorian chant's place in music history. Unfortunately for Pope Gregory I, he is most likely receiving undeserved credit, even though legend tells that the chants were revealed to him by the Holy Spirit (taking the form of a dove), and he then dictated and preserved the chants. Charlemagne and his successors spread Gregorian chant throughout their lands, and thus they unified the church (for the most part) through a common music.

One final repertory of chant that survived until the twelfth century is Old Roman Chant, which not surprisingly was the chant of the city of Rome. Although this dialect of chant essentially drew upon the same liturgies and texts as Gregorian chant, the Old Roman chants were often more ornate. Given their similarities, it is truly impossible to know with any certainty whether Gregorian chant begot Old Roman chant or vice-versa.

Aside from the body of liturgical musical literature that survives from the Middle Ages, probably the single most important development in musical history from this period was the invention of musical notation. Until this time, there was no unified approach to the written transmission of music; while the texts of eighth-century Roman liturgy were recorded on paper, the melodies that accompanied them were passed down through oral transmission. How these melodies were preserved and transmitted is greatly debated and somewhat controversial. While frequently sung melodies could likely have been passed down verbatim from generation to generation, it is unlikely that this was the case for the hundreds of chants that were sung infrequently. It is much more likely that variations appeared with each transmission and that the chants were improvised within established conventions.

As long as chant melodies survived only in the memories of those who sung and heard them, there undoubtedly would be changes or corruptions to the original tunes. The solution to this was notation, a means for writing down the music. In the earliest notations, small signs called *neumes* (derived from the Latin neuma, meaning "gesture") indicated the number of pitches per syllable and the ascent or descent of the melody. One important development in the eleventh-century was devised by a monk named Guido of Arezzo, who suggested a series of horizontal lines and spaces that would indicate given pitches. This system, now known as staff notation, gave rise to today's modern music notation. The only problem with this system is that it only could indicate pitch level, not rhythmic duration.

LINES AND DASHES, LINES AND DASHES, GO TOGETHER LIKE LOVE AND, AH, MARR ASH ?

GUIDO OF AREZZO

Jumping ahead about 800 years, the Benedictine monks of the Abbey of Solesmes France prepared modern editions of the chants, which was then proclaimed the official Vatican edition by Pope Pius X in 1903. While the Solesmes editions included dots and dashes to indicate lengthened note durations, the problem of notating rhythmic durations was not fully solved. Chant notation still assumed relatively equal rhythmic durations for each of the pitches (which were organized into groups of two and three), which had been the standard for the past 800 years.

Each of the chants was based on one of eight church modes, scales that indicated important features of the chant. The modes informed the chanter of the final (the most important note in the chant and usually the last note in the melody), the range of the chant, and the reciting tone (the second most important note in a mode, often emphasized in the chant and used for reciting text in a psalm). So how would one go about learning how to sing these chants?

Guido of Arezzo, in his infinite wisdom, devised a set of syllables that corresponded to the series of steps and half-steps in the church modes and used the syllables of the first six phrases of the hymn *Ut queant laxis: ut, re, mi, fa, sol,* and *la.* Sound familiar? It's the basis of today's modern solfege system, which millions have heard in "Do-Re-Mi" in the musical *The Sound of Music.* Guido's followers didn't stop there; they created a pedagogical aid called the "Guidonian Hand," to help singers learn to sing the intervals. The teacher would point to various joints of the open left hand, with a joint assigned to each of the twenty notes of the system.

From the codification of liturgical chants, to the development of a method for transcribing melodies, to the development of a solmization system for singing those melodies, the Middle Ages yielded a wealth of developments in music that have strongly influenced the development of music and notation in Western art music.

Chapter 3

THE ROMAN LITURGY

Just as the church was the primary vehicle for the composition of music throughout history, the mass was the single most important part of the Roman Liturgy for a number of reasons. For the Roman church, the Mass serves as the most important religious service, in the Middle Ages and the present day. The Mass is divided into two main parts or *liturgies:* The Liturgy of the Word and the Liturgy of the Eucharist. During the Liturgy of the Word, scriptures from the Old Testament, New Testament, and Gospels are read and pondered; The Liturgy of the Eucharist is a reenactment of the Last Supper of Jesus, with the priest assuming the role of Jesus by consecrating the bread and wine and transforming them into the body and blood of

Jesus. The consecrated elements are then offered to the faithful as communion. The Mass is celebrated every Sunday in all churches, in addition to special feast days (Christmas and Easter are the two most important); in monasteries, abbeys, convents, and major cathedrals, the Mass is celebrated daily.

Understanding the Mass[1] itself is important to those studying music, as it will remain one of the principle genres of music for the next 1,500 years! The texts of the Mass form the basis of many musical compositions, compositions that served a liturgical function and those that simply used the text as a genre without any liturgical function. The texts of the Mass are divided into two main parts as well, both parts appearing in both the Liturgy of the Word and the Liturgy of the Eucharist. The first main text, the Mass Ordinary, refers to those parts of the Mass that were the same at every celebration: *Kyrie, Gloria, Credo, Sanctus,* and *Agnus Dei.* The second main text, the Mass Proper, includes all texts that changed according to the church calendar (and thus were different at every single Mass): *Introit, Epistle, Gradual, Alleluia, Sequence, Offertory,* and *Communion.*

For those studying sacred music, it is most important to understand the function of the parts of the Mass Ordinary, the staples of each Mass. The *Kyrie* (which actually is Greek, not Latin!) is a threefold invocation at the beginning of the Mass, stating, "Lord, have mercy. Christ, have mercy. Lord, have mercy." You will notice that groups of three are incredibly common in sacred music, as it is usually a reference to the

---

[1] *When referring to the actual religious service,* Mass *is always capitalized; when referring to the set of texts used as a genre of musical composition,* mass *is not capitalized.*

threefold existence of God (the Holy Trinity) as God the Father, God the Son, and God the Holy Spirit. The *Gloria*, a text of praise that again asks for mercy, invokes the triune presence of God. The *Gloria* is never sung during the penitential seasons of Advent and Lent, nor in Masses that take place outside of Sundays and feast days.

The *Credo* (Latin for *creed*) is a statement of faith and belief in the church doctrine. At the center of the creed is a recounting of Jesus's suffering, death, and resurrection. The creed most commonly set to music is the Nicene Creed, although it is not uncommon in a Mass to hear the Apostles' Creed. Both are very similar to each other. In the Sanctus, the faithful join the angelic host in proclaiming "Holy, holy, holy, Lord God of Hosts!" The *Agnus Dei* (Lamb of God), like the *Kyrie,* is threefold in its structure: "Lamb of God, who takest away the sins of the world, have mercy on us (2 times); Lamb of God, who takest away the sins of the world, grant us peace."

It is important to remember that each of these parts of the Mass Ordinary was set to chant melodies, which can be described in one of three ways. The *Credo* and *Gloria* were typically **syllabic chants,** meaning that each syllable of text was set to only one pitch or neume. Both of the texts are quite lengthy, and a syllabic treatment of the texts was the most efficient manner for declaiming them. The *Sanctus* and *Agnus Dei,* with relatively shorter texts, were often **neumatic chants,** with one to six pitches set to each syllable of text. The *Kyrie* chants, with its brief, six-word text, were quite florid and were **melismatic chants,** which featured long melodic passages set to a single syllable of text.

The importance of chant in the development of music for the next millennium cannot be overstated. Chant will form the basis of the polyphonic music of the ninth through sixteenth centuries, it will be adapted by musicians during the Reformation as the basis of hymn tunes and chorales, and it will continue to play a role in musical composition (both in sacred and secular music) well into the twentieth century.

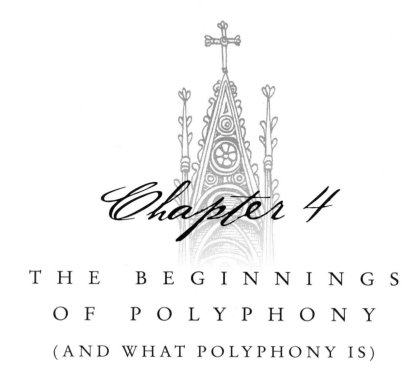

Chapter 4

THE BEGINNINGS

OF POLYPHONY

(AND WHAT POLYPHONY IS)

etween 1050 and 1300, a new style of architecture, later called Gothic, emerged in the construction of churches and cathedrals. The style featured ornate facades, towers, spires, large stained-glass windows, spacious vaults, and pointed arches. These same fanciful developments were also seen in art (in the form of paintings, sculptures, and manuscripts) and in music in the form of *polyphony.* In contrast to the single-voice melodies (monody) that had been the norm, polyphonic pieces of music were created for voices singing together in independent parts.

Polyphony began as a way of decorating existing chant by simply adding more voices, but it soon became valued as ornament or decoration by those who heard or sang it, making it a central piece of art music in the thirteenth century. Like the spacious vaults and stained-glass windows of church architecture, polyphony added to the grandeur and opulence of the liturgy itself. The development of polyphony was further enabled by simultaneous developments in musical notation (they found a few ways to notate rhythmic durations!).

At its inception and most basic form, it was likely common that voices or instruments performed in multiple parts before the advances in notation in polyphony. The simplest type of such polyphony occurred with the singing or playing of a melody against a drone, a sustained pitch (think bagpipes). One of the earliest forms of polyphony in church music was the *organum,* where one voice would sing the chant melody (the principal voice) and one or more voices would sing another melody in tandem (the organal voice or voices). In this genre, the voices weren't truly independent of one another: most frequently they moved in a note-for-note fashion (parallel organum). But in the case of florid organum, the organal voice would sing many notes in a melismatic fashion against a single note in the principle voice.

Ornate styles of polyphony flourished in Paris in the late twelfth and early thirteenth centuries, particularly in the new Cathedral of Paris known as Notre Dame (and yes, it too was constructed in the Gothic style). The complexity and magnificence of the music composed here was unrivaled anywhere else in the world, due largely in part that the majority of the music was notated rather than improvised.

One of the most important developments in music notation since Ancient Greece was the new-found ability to notate duration of pitches, an incredibly important advancement in notation for later music. Combinations of note groups called ligatures were used to indicate different patterns of short notes (called breves) and long notes (called longs). Altogether, there were six basic patterns of note groups that have become known as rhythmic modes. You might recall that there were already established church modes to define particular collections of pitches in chant. Now we have modes to distinguish particular groupings of rhythm!

The two principle composers at Notre Dame that left an indelible mark on Notre Dame polyphony and notation were Léonin and Pérotin. Léonin is credited with compiling the *Magnus liber organi* ("great book of polyphony"), in which is contained two-voice settings of portions of chants for the most important feast days of the church year. Although the great book no longer exists in its original form, the majority of its content exists in the form of extant manuscripts in Germany and Italy. Pérotin built on Léonin's work by editing

the *Magnus liber* and supplementing the organa with additional voices, often adding a third or even fourth voice. Through these additions, Pérotin managed to create some of the most sophisticated music to date, music even more magnificent than that of Léonin.

With the introduction of polyphony to liturgical music in the thirteenth century, new forms and genres of vocal music arose, the most important being the **motet.** The Latin term *motetus,* from the French *mot* meaning "word," came to encompass vocal works that featured newly written Latin texts added to existing music. The motet saw rapid changes and developments, from the inclusion of French language (instead of Latin) to the use of secular topics to the eventual freedom from the established rhythmic modes. The motet is a genre and form of music that will continue to flourish well into the twentieth century, albeit with drastic and radical developments along the way. Not only did motets of this time feature multiple independent voices, but these voices often had completely different texts being sung simultaneously! For example, a triple motet featured three independent voices singing independent notes and text over a fourth voice (called the tenor) that sang a fixed line of music (called the *cantus firmus*) in long rhythmic durations.

For the first time in music history, note durations were finally being indicated by the shapes of the notes, which is a characteristic Western music has held onto ever since. Around 1280, Franco of Cologne created this new system of notation that had four principle rhythmic values for notes: the double long, the long, the breve,

HEY, COMPOSERS, THIS'LL PUT A LITTLE BREVE IN YOUR BRIEFS.

and the semibreve, each half the length of the preceding one. Today, we still use a notation system of whole notes, half notes, quarter notes, and eighth notes (again, each note value half the length of the preceding one.) This new notational system, called Franconian notation, allowed for composers to liberate themselves from the rhythmic modes, leading to both innovation and variety in the composition of motets.

In just a few hundred years, classical music saw huge strides in terms of musical composition. In the year 1000, music consisted essentially of a single melody line; by 1300, polyphonic compositions consisting of multiple independent voices became the norm, although new monophonic music did not fade away entirely. And two major innovations in music notation (rhythmic modes and Franconian notation) allowed more information about the duration of pitches to be written down. As you will read in the next chapter, many more innovations in musical notation and form are yet to come in the fourteenth century.

Chapter 5

MUSIC IN THE FOURTEENTH CENTURY FRANCE AND ITALY

In contrast to the stable and prosperous thirteenth century, the 1300s were a tumultuous time for Europe. Over the course of the century, Europeans were plagued by war (the Hundred Years' War); famine brought about by flooding in northwestern Europe; reduced agricultural production caused by climate changes; and disease (the Black Death, a combination of pneumonic and bubonic plagues that decimated about a third of the population). The Church, which had long been a unifying force across Europe, faced problems of its own: the election of French Pope Clement V, who remained in Avignon instead of residing in Rome, was known as the Babylonian Captivity, with the popes essentially serving as puppets of the French monarchy. This was then followed by the Great Schism, with rival "popes" in Rome, Avignon, and later in Pisa.

Music, then, sought a balance between structure and pleasure—a way of counteracting the uncertainty, turmoil, and misery in the other aspects of European life at the time. Structure was introduced in the forms of new rhythmic and melodic patterning and the standardization of song forms; and pleasure through the composition of more interesting and engaging melodies and harmonies, with innovations in rhythm and meter. One of the leading innovators of the time was Philippe de Vitry (1291-1361) who pioneered a "new art": the **Ars Nova,** a Latin term that refers to this new French musical style in the fourteenth century.

The Ars Nova featured two main innovations in rhythm and musical notation. In regards to rhythm, the "new art" allowed for two different divisions of any note value: the "imperfect" double division along with the long-standing "perfect" triple division. Additionally, the semibreve (which previously was the smallest possible rhythmic duration) could now be divided further into *minims.* Around the middle of the century, the Ars Nova began incorporation **mensuration signs,** symbols placed at the beginning of music that indicated the rhythmic and metric profile of the music and which are the ancestors of today's modern time signatures.

By far the most important composer in the fourteenth century was Guillaume de Machaut (ca. 1300-1377), who, under the patronage of the aristocracy and royalty, produced a body of musical compositions numbering nearly 140. Machaut collected his work into manuscripts which he prepared for his patrons, marking a shift in self-awareness of musicians as artists in their own right—prior to this, anonymity was the norm. Machaut composed in nearly every genre of music, from masses to motets to secular songs.

GUILLAUME DE MACHAUT

Machaut composed both secular and sacred song, although his composition of motets dates primarily to the early part of his career. His motets continued in the established style of multiple voices above a cantus firmus, although were rhythmically more complex than those of his predecessors. Machaut, who was also a poet, composed a number of secular songs, mostly on the subject of love. The most popular genres of secular song came from the *formes fixes* (fixed forms), which prescribed particular patterns of repetition for both the text and the music. These formes fixes applied not only to monophonic songs, but also to the newly developed polyphonic songs known as *chansons* (French for "songs"). All of the fixed forms derived their forms from genres associated with dancing.

Machaut's most significant contribution to the musical canon is his *Messe de Nostre Dame* (Mass of Our Lady), which is one of the earliest known polyphonic settings of the Mass Ordinary. Additionally, it is most likely the first polyphonic mass to have been composed entirely by a single composer and conceived of as a cohesive musical unit. Previously, polyphonic settings of mass movements could easily be combined with various other settings in a service. Machaut, in contrast, treats the six movements of his mass as a single composition. Machaut received high regard as a poet and composer by his contemporaries and for several decades after his death, and his works are a large part of the canon of that time because he ensured their survival through carefully preserved and numerous manuscripts.

France and Italy in the Middle Ages were very distinct countries; France, for instance, was ruled by a monarch, while Italy was a collection of city-states, each with its own distinct dialect, culture, and political system. Despite these differences, the music of France did have a significant impact on Italian composers in the later part of the fourteenth century. Italian composers

25

lost more of their specific regional characteristics and absorbed the new styles of French music. Italians set their music to French texts and used French forms. In fact, even manuscripts of Italian compositions were sometimes notated in French!

Despite the French influence on Italian musical compositions, Italian *Trecento* music (which comes from the Italian "mille trecento" for 1300) produced innovations in its own right. While French composers made their mark in both sacred and secular forms, Trecento music thrived primarily in the form of secular polyphonic songs. Church polyphony at the time was mostly improvised, and very little Italian church music actually survives in manuscript. The polyphonic songs of the Italian Trecento, which like the French were composed as entertainment for the aristocracy, were preserved and survive in much greater numbers.

The fourteenth-century *madrigal* was a song for two or three voices to be sung unaccompanied by instruments. In the next section, we'll take a look at the sixteenth-century madrigal, which was a completely different genre of music (and much more well-known than its earlier counterpart). The Trecento madrigal features all voices singing the same text, usually one that was pastoral, satirical, or amorous in nature. Each stanza of the madrigal was closed with a refrain called a ***ritornello*** (this term will reappear throughout the development of classical music and serve in very different roles). Unlike the French Ars Nova (where the melody in one voice dominated the others), the voices in Trecento madrigals were essentially equal, with no one voice dominating.

The leading Trecento composer was Francesco Landini (ca. 1325-1397), who composed a host of secular songs, in particular the very popular *ballata.* The word *ballata* comes from the Italian verb *ballare* ("to dance"), and seems to have been influenced by the French chanson style, in which the melody in one voice predominated. Landini composed around 140 ballate, which were originally intended to accompany dancing. He also composed 12 madrigals and a couple of songs in other forms, thus demonstrating the overwhelming popularity of the ballata.

FRANCESCO LANDINI

In hindsight, the French and Italian composers of the fourteenth century made significant contributions to the development of both sacred and secular art music. Unfortunately, their music did not have much staying power at the time, replaced with the innovations of the fifteenth century and with much of it unperformed for centuries until the music's rediscovery in the twentieth century.

II

A REBIRTH:

MUSIC OF THE

RENAISSANCE

CHAPTER 6

T H E   M U S I C A L
R E N A I S S A N C E

*I*n the fifteenth and sixteenth century, we see great changes
and advances in European culture, literature, art, and music. These changes, however, did not all take place simultaneously to
form a singular new style; rather, the changes were constant, continually
overlapping one another. More and more composers began taking positions outside of their native countries, leading to an internationalization
of musical styles within compositions. A renewed interest in ancient
Greek theory and ideals led to a stronger focus on the words of songs
themselves: setting music with a proper declamation of the text and a
consideration for the emotion and meaning of the text being set.

The humanist movement (the term comes from the Latin *studia
humanitatis,* the study of the humanities) was by the single most
influential intellectual movement of the Renaissance. **Humanism** was

a revival of ancient thought, philosophy, and learning, and the interest in the study of grammar, rhetoric, poetry, history, and moral philosophy stemmed from the renewed interest in classical Latin and Greek writings. In art and music, artists also turned to classical models in their own artistic and musical creations, with beauty, structure, and naturalism being important influences. Humanism did not contradict or undermine the role and prominence of the Church; rather, humanism worked alongside Christian doctrine to bolster people's minds, spirits, and ethics so that they might lead lives of virtue and service.

The development of music in the Renaissance paralleled the humanist movement. Prior to the fifteenth century, it was uncommon to consider a composer having a unique personal compositional style, but as the Renaissance developed, the artist in his own right became the norm. Composers sought clarity and structure in their music, expanded the range of pitches used in their compositions, and employed more contrast in their works (sections with many high pitches versus many low pitches, sections with full textures—many voices—and sections with sparse textures—fewer voices).

Musicians' training, employment, and travels were key to the development of music in the Renaissance. An increase in musical institutions and patronage created an unprecedented number of opportunities for musicians. Court chapels became the most common form of patronage, where groups of paid musicians and clerics regularly composed, entertained, and performed for a particular ruler (as opposed to being confined to music-making in a single building). These chapel musicians provided music not only for church services, but also for the entertainment of the court. Like having the finest garments and the most opulent palaces, rulers sought to have the most excellent music, which was both enjoyable and, conveniently, a demonstration of the rulers' wealth and power.

Aside from providing a place for the creation and performance of new music, the court chapels brought together musicians from a host of various regions. This, in turn, led to the development of increasingly cosmopolitan musicians. English, French and Italian musical traditions coalesced and synthesized into new internationalized styles of music because of the constant exchange of regional and national traditions, genres, and ideas. Later in the Renaissance, the cosmopolitan musician will not only be able to compose music in his own nationalistic styles, but also in the styles of other regions. Italian composers will write French chanson, and German composers will write Italian madrigals.

Along with changes in regional styles of composition, new methods and textures of composition also developed during the Renaissance. As mentioned previously, most polyphonic compositions focused on a higher, melodic voice superimposed upon a fixed line of existing music. In the Renaissance, composers moved toward greater equality of voices, paid more attention to the dissonances created by vertical sonorities (and avoided them), and sought to make each individual voice part interesting and gratifying to sing.

As mentioned earlier in this chapter, there was also a renewed interest in Greek theory, philosophy and ideals. The Pythagorean tuning system (remember, simple ratios of 2:1, 3:2, and 4:3 were perfectly tuned) served medieval music well, as only perfect fourths, fifth and octaves needed to sound in-tune; unfortunately, this meant that all other intervals[2] were severely out of tune. With a great interest in new consonant sonorities, it became necessary to devise new tuning systems to allow a greater number of intervals to sound in-tune. One solution was *just intonation,* where the major third and minor third intervals were considered consonances, with their ratios approaching 5:4 and 6:5. The problem with this tuning system is that while some fourths, fifths, and thirds sounded in tune, others must be out of tune. First described in the late 1500s, *equal temperament* became the standard tuning system (and still is today), with each semitone being exactly the same distance from the next semitone. The result of this is that thirds, fourths, and fifths are ever-so-slightly out of tune, with the octave being the only perfectly tuned interval.

OY! I GOTTA TUNE THIS THING.

---

[2] *An interval is the distance between two notes that sound either simultaneously (harmonically) or sequentially (melodically). The vertical sonorities that composers are concerning themselves with are based upon the harmonic intervals created when multiple voices are singing simultaneously.*

While people in the Renaissance could easily experience ancient art, poetry, and architecture, they unfortunately could not experience ancient music. Ancient Greek writings, however, were able to give people of the Renaissance insight into the ideals of ancient music, and those writings influenced Renaissance musical compositions and music in society. In ancient Greek society, music was a requirement of every person's education—educated persons were expected to be able to read music, sing music at sight, and take part in group forms of music-making. The ancient Greeks also saw an inseparable relationship between poetry and music. In the Renaissance, this translated to composers paying much closer attention to the organization and syntax of the text they were setting. They also placed importance on following the natural rhythm, pacing, and accentuation of the text. Previously singers had the freedom to sing the words as they sought fit, but Renaissance composers took back control of this aspect of music, insisting that the music serve the words and not the other way around. Composers also aimed to capture the emotional and expressive content of the poetry through careful use of specific intervals, melodic contours, and textures.

The development of movable type and music printing in the Renaissance proved to be one of the most important advancements in the production, duplication, and distribution of music to the masses. Perfected around 1450 by Johann Gutenberg, movable type allowed for notes to be assembled in any order, rearranged, and reused, and it was much more practical (and

PRETTY SOON EVERYONE WIL BE SINGING MY SONG.

JOHANN GUTENBERG

AND NOW EVERYONE CAN SING EVERYONE ELSE'S SONG, TOO!

time-efficient) than carving music into wood blocks or copying musical manuscripts by hand. Ottaviano Petrucci, a Venetian businessman, published the first collection of polyphonic music in 1501. The ability to print music led to the production of *partbooks*—each partbook contained the music for a single voice, and a complete set was needed (one for each voice) in order to perform a musical work. Partbooks, due to printed music now being much more affordable, were owned in homes for music-making at social gatherings and in church choirs. Both supply and demand for printed music increased, resulting in competition among the numerous music publishers that popped up in the sixteenth century.

The developments in music in the Renaissance had a profound and lasting effect on music for centuries. Sixteenth-century music continued to have appeal well into the seventeenth and eighteenth centuries, with a revival in interest in the late nineteenth- and early twentieth centuries. Technological developments in the printing process made musical scores accessible to many more people, and advances in tuning systems became the foundation of the tuning systems employed in music to this day.

Chapter 7

JOSQUIN: THE NEXT GENERATION

any composers in the Renaissance contributed to developments and innovation in music, so many that it is beyond the scope of this book to identify and discuss all of them! This chapter is dedicated to several Franco-Flemish composers born around the middle of the fifteenth century who represent a significant shift in the compositional styles of the Renaissance. Three of the most prolific composers of the late fifteenth and early sixteenth centuries were Jacob Obrecht (1457 or 1458-1505), Heinrich Isaac (ca. 1450-1517), and the estimable Josquin des Prez (ca. 1450-1521). These three had illustrious international careers, and the cosmopolitan nature of their lives is reflected in their music, a combination of both French and Italian characteristics.

The music of Obrecht, Isaac, and Josquin (known by his given name because "des Prez" was a nickname) shared a number of elements of style. The chosen text for a piece of music now largely determined the musical form of vocal works. Individual voice parts in polyphonic works focused on singability and having nearly equal importance among all parts. The tenor (which previously held the cantus firmus) was replaced in this generation by the bass, the lowest sounding voice, as the foundation of harmony. The Franco-Flemish composers still borrowed melodies from both secular and sacred sources, but they tended to distribute the melody among all voices instead of committing it to a single voice. The mass and the motet remained the most significant forms of musical composition, and this generation of composers broke away from the formes fixes that predominated in the early Renaissance.

Jacob Obrecht composed about 28 motets, 30 masses, and a number of secular songs and instrumental pieces. Obrecht's contribution to the development of polyphonic music is his extensive use of imitation in his works. Earlier in the Renaissance, imitation between voices (where one or more voices would echo the same melody as the first entering voice) was not very common. Obrecht changed this, with many of his works focusing on points of imitation, a series of imitative entrances by the vocal forces.

Heinrich Isaac, too, was a major player in the music world at the turn of the fourteenth and fifteenth centuries. Isaac was employed by two of the most famous and important patrons in Europe. From 1484 to 1492 he served as a composer and singer for Lorenzo de' Medici in Florence, and beginning in 1497, he  served as the court composer for Holy Roman Emperor Maximilian I at Vienna and Innsbruck. Sacred music was his niche, with Isaac producing an incredible output of 35 masses, 50 motets, and the *Choralis Constantinus,* a prolific compendium of musical settings of the text and melodies of the Mass Proper for most of the church year. Isaac is known for his use of both polyphonic and **homophonic**[3] textures, often alternating between the two textures within a song or mass movement.

There are not many composers who have experienced the renown, respect, or influence than Josquin de Prez. Josquin worked in the most prestigious courts and churches in France and Italy, and his motets, masses, and songs were revered, performed, and imitated both during his lifetime and for nearly a century after his death (a rarity in a time when music more than 20-30 years old was deemed old-fashioned and not worthy of performance). Further proving Josquin's relative fame, Petrucci published three books of Josquin's masses with numerous reprints to meet demand; in contrast, no other composer had more than a single volume of music published by Petrucci. In 1538, Reformation leader Martin Luther declared this about Josquin and his music: "Josquin is the master of the notes. They must do as he wills; as for the other composers, they have to do as the notes will." All of this reflects not only on the importance of Josquin himself, but also on the composer as an individual artist.

The more than fifty motets composed by Josquin demonstrate his unique style and the free composition, clarity in form, tuneful melodies, and use of both imitation and homophony already in use

THANKS FOR THE ENDORSEMENT, MARTY.

MARTIN LUTHER   JOSQUIN DES PREZ

---

[3] *Homophonic textures are described as settings where the voices move in the same rhythm with the same text simultaneously; the voices are not independent of each other as they are in polyphonic music. A good example of homophonic music in today's culture would be the church hymn written in four parts.*

in the late-fifteenth-century. Josquin's renown comes mostly from his treatment of the texts, aiming to reflect the meaning of words through **text depiction** (instances where the music aims to paint an aural image of the words) and through **text expression** (where the overall musical work seeks to convey the emotional content of the words). The philosophy that music could convey extramusical meaning such as emotions was a common one for the ancient Greeks. But between antiquity and the late fifteenth century, this philosophy seemed to have been lost on composers of music—if they did attempt to convey emotion through music, they did so in a way that we cannot understand.

Josquin excelled not only in his composition of motets, but also in the ingenuity of his masses. His masses drew from a genre of masses called mass cycles. Mass cycles use five sections of the Mass Ordinary (*Kyrie, Gloria, Credo, Sanctus,* and *Agnus Dei*) as the five movements of the composition. While earlier masses created a musical link between two movements, the mass cycle of the fifteenth century unifies all of the movements with some type of recurring musical material. Earlier mass cycles used a single melody as the beginning pitches in one or all voices (called a **motto mass**), or a recurring melody in one voice (called a **cantus-firmus mass**). Josquin was innovative in that he based his masses on all voices of the borrowed musical material, such as a motet or chanson.

39

Imitating another polyphonic work, the *imitation mass* became one of Josquin's crowning achievements. In instances where he did use a single melody as the unifying musical device, he paraphrased the tune in all of the voices (not just in a single voice), creating what is now known as a *paraphrase mass.* If you are thinking that these two types of masses would sound the same, you're right! The only difference between the two masses is the music they borrow from: the imitation mass borrows from a polyphonic work (such as a motet), while the paraphrase mass borrows from a monophonic source (such as a chant).

The fifteenth century represented a time for both the old and the new. The formes fixes reached their climax in this century and were eventually abandoned for free compositional forms. The vocal ranges of music expanded greatly, voices gained greater independence and equality simultaneously, imitation became increasingly common, and the treatment of borrowed musical material grew in freedom. Josquin and his generation shifted focus to the text, in form, declamation, depiction, and expression. The new technology of music printing cemented Josquin's place in the music history books as one of the greatest composers of his generation and possibly of the entire Renaissance.

Chapter 8

THE REFORMATION
AND ITS EFFECT
ON MUSIC

At the beginning of the sixteenth century, nearly all of Europe was united by a single Catholic Church, which was centered in Rome and supported by political leaders across the continent. By the middle of the century, this unified belief system that had existed since the Middle Ages was no longer intact. Beginning as merely a theological dispute, the Reformation exploded into a full-out rebellion against the Catholic Church, starting in Germany with Martin Luther, then spreading to most of northern Europe. The Calvinist movement, headed by Jean Calvin, swept across Switzerland and the Low Countries to France and Britain, while the politically-motivated Church of England began to take hold in much of England, with King Henry VIII at the helm.

While Martin Luther (1483-1546) had a number of theological qualms with the teachings of the Catholic Church, we will only examine the philosophies that had the greatest impact on music in the church during the Reformation. Luther felt that the people needed to play a larger role in the church he had created. One principle way to create a sense of inclusion was to limit the amount of Latin in the service, with the majority of the service spoken in the vernacular, the language of the people. He did keep some Latin in the services, as he thought it important for the education of youth. Despite the uproar he caused with his Reformation, Luther, in fact, kept much of the Catholic liturgy intact in the Lutheran service! Lutheran churches continued to employ Catholic chants and polyphony, although the texts were sometimes changed to German translations or entirely new German words.

I WILL OUT-CATHOLIC THE CATHOLICS AND I'LL DO IT WITH THE PEOPLE — NOW THAT'S A REFORMATION!

Luther himself was a musician; therefore it follows that music would play a central role in the Lutheran service. He was a composer, an instrumentalist, and a singer, and as noted in the previous chapter, he greatly admired the polyphonic music of Franco-Flemish composers, especially Josquin. Likewise, he held a deep admiration for the Greek philosophy of the ethical and emotional power of music. Luther believed that through communal (congregational) singing, worshipers would be united in their faith and praise of God. This was a contradiction of Catholic customs, where normally only the celebrants and the choir would perform music in worship services.

The most important musical form to come from the Lutheran Church (and the Reformation, for that matter) was the congregation hymn, known as the *chorale* since the late 1500s. Like many Protestant services today, worshipers would sing several chorales congregationally throughout a worship service. While known today as four-part harmonized hymns, chorales in Luther's day consisted only of a single melody based on a metered, rhymed, and strophic poem without harmonization or accompaniment. Creating an entire body of music for worship throughout the church year in a short amount of time would be no easy feat, and so the Lutherans looked to a number of sources to quickly assimilate their canon of sacred music. In addition to new compositions, the three main sources for chorales were existing German devotional songs, adaptations of Gregorian chant, and secular songs given new words (a practice called *contrafactum*). Aside from saving an immense amount of time composing entirely new music, use of existing Catholic music in new ways drew a connection to the past and asserted Lutheranism as part of a long-standing Christian faith. All told, the Lutheran church had more than 700 chorale melodies in its body of service of music by the year 1600.

The second largest form of Protestantism (second only to Lutheranism) was the Calvinist movement, led by Jean Calvin (1509-1564). He shared some beliefs with the Lutherans, such as rejecting papal authority, but asserted many of his own beliefs, including the belief that all people are predestined for either salvation or damnation. His church spread across Europe, resulting in the Presbyterian church in Scotland and the Puritans in England. The most important aspect of Calvinism is the belief that worship should focus on God alone. Thus, Calvinists stripped their church of all things superfluous, distracting, or ornamental: decorative paintings, sculptures, stained-glass windows, instruments, and polyphonic music were all banned from the church.

IF WE HAVE TO HAVE MUSIC MAKE IT A PSALM.

JEAN CALVIN

In contrast to Luther who used various non-scriptural texts in music, Calvin asserted that only biblical texts, particularly the psalms, be sung in the church. Psalms, of course, are not uniform in length, making singing them quite difficult for congregations. Calvin's solution to this was the *metrical psalm*—rhymed, metered, strophic psalms that had been translated into the vernacular and set to new melodies or existing chant tunes. These metrical psalms were then collected and published in books called psalters.

The third major branch of the Protestant movement in the sixteenth century was the Church of England, a politically motivated creation by King Henry VIII after disagreements with the pope in regards to his marital situation with Catherine of Aragon. Church music changed drastically in the Church of England. New musical forms were created for the church services, now in English, although the monarchy still allowed some composition of Latin motets and masses. Queen Elizabeth I placed value in the tradition of Latin sacred polyphony, and so she still allowed the use of Latin in some churches. John Taverner (ca.1490-1545) and Thomas Tallis (1505-1585) were important composers in the early and middle parts of the century, but William Byrd (1540-1623) was the eminent English composer in the late Renaissance.

HENRY VIII

Byrd composed a host of Anglican church music, from Great Services, to psalms, to full anthems, but he is best known for his Latin masses and motets. Despite the religious revolution mandated by the royal family, Byrd remained a staunch Catholic, which at the time was an act of treason and punishable by death. He wrote many of his works for liturgical use by Catholics who celebrated Mass clandestinely. Fortunately for Byrd, he was protected by Queen Elizabeth from prosecution because he was a loyal subject and servant to her. Byrd's split allegiances between the Catholic Church and the Church of England, embodied in his dual output of Catholic and Anglican music, were representative of the larger religious divisions across Europe.

NO MORE PROFANE POLYPHONY.

In response to the Protestant Reformation, the Catholic Church initiated a number of measures known as the Counter-Reformation. The Council of Trent (1545-1563) proclaimed most of these initiatives, going so far as to recommend a ban on most polyphonic music in Mass: "Let them keep away from the churches compositions in which there is an intermingling of the lascivious or impure, whether by instrument or by voice." In essence, the Council declared that polyphony was prohibited except in instances when the words were unobscured and comprehensible to all. Giovanni Pierluigi da Palestrina (1525 or 1526-1594), the leading Italian composer of church music at the time, is regarded with having rescued polyphony from condemnation. Legend tells that he composed a six-voice mass (known as the *Pope Marcellus Mass*) in which the music was reverent and the words unobscured.

BUT WAIT 'TIL YOU HEAR THIS, BOYS!

PALESTRINA

Palestrina has been referred to as the "Prince of Music" and his compositions the epitome of perfection in church music. He composed more than 104 mass settings, as well as a number of motets. His style is marked by tuneful, elegant, and easily singable melodies, discreet treatment of dissonance, and careful attention to text setting with subtle text depiction. Palestrina's style of composition was carefully preserved and then studied by future generations, eventually serving as the quintessential model of the stile antico (old style) for seventeenth-century composers and scholars.

Chapter 9

MADRIGALS

(THEY AREN'T ALWAYS

ACCOMPANIED BY DINNERS)

AND OTHER

SECULAR SONGS

While the battle over religion (and the musical consequences of the Reformation) was raging across Europe in the sixteenth century, musicians were busy fostering new secular musical forms with their own nationalistic styles and identities. The interplay between poetry and music became increasingly important, especially in regards to realizing fully the emotional, visual, and accentual content of the poetry being set to music. The technological breakthrough in printing in 1501 provided additional impetus for the composition and dissemination of secular song across Europe in the sixteenth century.

Secular song took many forms in the sixteenth century, with style, form, and name dominated by the particular region in which the composer lived. In Spain the *villancico* became the predominant song form; its Italian counterpart was the *frottola.* The French continued composing their chansons, and both the Italians and the English composed the well-known madrigal. Music played an important part in the royal court of Ferdinand and Isabella in Spain, and they promoted the creation of a uniquely Spanish musical genre to help unify their country. The villancico was a short, strophic song usually on a rustic or popular topic. While the form might vary from one villancico to another, they all consisted of a refrain and one or more stanzas. They often would have a contrasting section, followed by a concluding iteration of the refrain. The tune was nearly always placed in the highest voice part, with other parts optionally sung or played on instruments below it. Many villancicos were published in collections to be sung by a solo voice and accompanied by a lute.

FERDINAND & ISABELLA

The Italian frottola was very similar to the Spanish villancico: it was a strophic song that was set mostly syllabically with the melody in the uppermost voice. Also like the villancico, the frottola was usually sung by a single voice, with the other voices played on instruments. While not rustic or popular in subject, the frottola generally featured simple music set to earthy or satirical texts. These frottole were quite fashionable in the Italian courts, resulting in composition of the genre nearly exclusively by Italian composers.

The most enduring song form to come from sixteenth-century Italy was the madrigal, and arguably the most important genre of the Renaissance. Its role in music history is bolstered by an increasingly heightened sensitivity to the meaning and impact of the text in composers' musical settings. Composers placed unprecedented emphasis on expressing every nuance of the poetic text. The expressivity, drama, and imagery of the madrigal not only established Italy as a musical leader in Western music, but also set the stage for the future development of dramatic music such as opera.

The formes fixes that had dominated for several hundred years were now a thing of the past. Recall that the formes fixes were just that: music and poetic lines were repeated in specified patterns. Even the villancico and frottola were strophic (repeated music for each strophe of poetry). But the madrigal was through-composed, meaning that new music was composed for every line of poetry. The poetry used for madrigals came from a variety of sources, from sonnets to freer poetic forms. Major poets were often the source for madrigals,

I MAY BE ITALY'S GREATEST POET BUT YOU'RE NOT A ROCK STAR UNTIL YOU WRITE A SONG.

PETRARCH

including the famous Petrarch (Francesco Petrarca, 1304-1374). Composers of madrigals (called madrigalists) aimed to recreate the ideas, images, and emotions of the poetry as vividly as possible. The earliest madrigals were written for four voices (here voices should be taken literally, one singer per voice part), later expanding to five voices and then six or more. These madrigals were exceedingly popular in Italian culture, with singers often performing them for their own enjoyment, as well as for the enjoyment of others in social gatherings, after meals, and in meetings of the academic community.

The madrigal's influence was not confined to the borders of Italy. Transcripts of Italian manuscripts eventually made their way to England, which motivated English composers to try their hand at writing in the style, in the hopes of making a profit. The other important song form to originate in sixteenth-century England was the lute song, a solo song with instrumental accompaniment (usually a lute). While not nearly as expressive in the text declamation, the lute song aimed to capture the overall emotion of the text, which was usually of a much more personal nature.

The madrigal truly brought Italy to the forefront of musical composition in Western Europe, and Italy would continue to be a leader throughout the upcoming Baroque era. As mentioned before, the painstaking attention to text depiction and text expression reached new heights, and eventually paved the way for even more dramatic text setting, such as opera. While madrigals themselves varied in popularity, it is certain that they had a profound and lasting impact on vocal music.

Chapter 10

STRIKE UP
THE BAND:
INSTRUMENTAL MUSIC
TAKES THE STAGE

*U*p until now, we have focused exclusively on vocal music, as the vast majority of music that was written down until the sixteenth century was indeed vocal music, sometimes with accompanying instruments. Of course, instrumental music was not absent from society; rather it was generally only used in fanfares or to accompany dancing, and not so much for pure listening or playing. Cultivation of instrumental music by churches and patrons increased significantly in the 1500s, and this is reflected in the preservation and dissemination (aided by printing) of instrumental music from this era and through the creation of new instruments.

FINALLY, TIME TO STRIKE UP THE BAND.

Instrumental music in the Renaissance played a role in a variety of cultural situations, from public or religious ceremonies, to entertainment for social gatherings, to accompaniment to dancing. Generally speaking, instrumental music composed in the Renaissance can be divided into five categories: dance music, arrangements of vocal music, arrangements of existing melodies, variations, and abstract instrumental works.

Dancing was one of the highlights of European society in the Renaissance, and knowledge of dance was expected of those in the upper social classes. In addition to improvising tunes or playing them from memory, instrumentalists also played from printed collections that were published for instrumental groups, lute, or keyboard[4]. Published dance movement served one of two purposes in the Renaissance. One, dance music written for ensembles (groups of players) was functional in that it simply accompanied dancers. Two, dances pieces for solo lute or keyboard were intended for the enjoyment of the player and/or those listening to the music. Dance music for ensembles was usually simple, with a melody played by a single instrument and accompanied by the rest, while solo dance music was highly stylized, often featuring ornamental and decorative flourishes. In any case, dance music conformed to preexisting dance forms that dictated that a particular meter, tempo, rhythmic pattern, and form be followed.

---

[4] *In the Renaissance, the principal keyboard instrument was the harpsichord. The harpsichord has one or multiple keyboards called manuals, and pitches were created by a small quill plucking a string when a key was depressed. In comparison, the modern piano creates sound by striking a string with a small hammer.*

Paradoxically, another principal source of instrumental music was existing vocal music. While it was previously common for instruments to double the voices of singers in the performance of vocal music, it became increasingly common in the sixteenth century for instrumental ensembles to play vocal music without any voices at all! Keyboardists and lutists, too, would play arrangements of vocal works, either improvising them or playing them from a published manuscript called an *intabulation.*

Like the vocal music we've examined to this point (such as the imitation mass), instrumental music also incorporated existing melodies in new compositions. It was common for church organists in particular to improvise or compose music based on Gregorian chants or other liturgical melodies. In the Lutheran church, they used German chorales as the source material. Many times, the verses of chorales would alternate between congregational singing and a setting for choir or organ, with organists typically improvising their verses of the chorale.

The ability to improvise on a tune was considered a valuable skill, and the ability to do so while accompanying dancing incredibly important. *Variations* was the style of improvisation most common during the sixteenth century. An instrumentalist would begin by starting with a specific melody, either existing or newly composed. Then, without any pause or interruption, the instrumentalist would play a series of variations of that theme. This style of instrumental music was useful in creating fresh, interesting takes on existing music, as well as demonstrating the skill and virtuosity of the performer.

While the first four categories of instrumental music are based on vocal or dance music, composers did write abstract instrumental works, instrumental compositions to be played or listened to for their own sake. The principal form of keyboard music written in an improvisatory style was the *toccata* (from the Italian *toccare*, "to touch"). The name served to remind the listener that the music was being created by an actual person. Other forms of abstract instrumental music include the *ricercare* (from the Italian "to seek out"), whose music was imitative and motetlike, and the canzon.

A chapter on instrumental music in the Renaissance would not be complete without mentioning Giovanni Gabrieli (ca.1555-1612). Gabrieli served as a church musician in the glorious St. Mark's Basilica in Venice. His compositions represent the glory of Venetian church music (particularly for the grandiose basilica), with many of his works to be performed by multiple choirs or instrumental ensembles. This genre of composition for multiple choirs was called polychoral motets. Music for divided choirs was not uncommon before Gabrieli, but he took the performing forces to new heights, often writing music for as many as five choirs of different vocal and instrumental timbres. Sometimes, these choirs would be divided spatially as well, perhaps with choirs in the two organ lofts, one on each side of the altar, and yet another choir on the floor.

ONE LUTE? NO, TWO, FIVE, A HUNDRED!

GIOVANNI GABRIELI

Regardless of the impetus or occasion for the composition, instrumental music in the sixteenth century took the stage in a major way, setting the scene for future instrumental works including the seventeenth-century sinfonia and the eighteenth-century symphony.

THE BAROQUE

PERIOD :

THE MUSIC OF

BACH & VIVALDI

Chapter 11

T H E   B E G I N N I N G S
O F   A   N E W   S T Y L E

IF IT AIN'T *BAROQUE* THEN DON'T FIX IT.

Between the years of 1600 and 1750, a period later referred to as the **Baroque** period, history sees significant developments in music, art, and architecture. Originally, the term *baroque*, originally from the Portuguese *barroco* for "misshapen pearl," meant abnormal, exaggerated, bizarre, or even being bad in taste. It was a negative term applied by critics in the mid-1700s who preferred the earlier styles of the Renaissance. In the mid-nineteenth century, the term took on a more positive connotation, as critics began to appreciate the dramatic, ornate, and expressive characteristics of the arts during the Baroque. As was the case with music of the Renaissance, the 150-year span of the Baroque encompassed a wide range of styles and musical developments.

Remember the doctrine of affections discussed in Chapter 1? In the Baroque, composers gave the strongest push towards the emotional qualities of music since antiquity. Composers sought, through music, to arouse the affections of listeners. These affections, or emotions, ranged from sadness, to joy, to anger, to excitement. These affections were caused by spirits, or "humors," in the body. By bringing these emotional states into harmony, persons would enjoy both physical and psychological health. Use of contrasting affects in music, then, would aid in realizing this balance of the affections. Music in the Baroque did not seek to express the composer's personal feelings, but rather sought to portray affections generically. In vocal music, composers aimed to capture the emotions, character, and drama of the text.

One of the defining characteristics of the early Baroque was the development of a second practice *(seconda prattica).* The *prima prattica,* or "first practice," referenced the sixteenth-century style of polyphony that we have just learned about in the past few chapters. The first practice focused on the rules that musical composition must follow, with a model of music dominating the text. The second practice, in contrast, placed even more emphasis on conveying the meaning and emotion of the text. This, in turn, led to the breaking of established rules of composition, introducing more dissonance into music to more convincingly convey the feelings and meaning of the text. It is important to note that the seconda prattica did not replace the prima prattica; rather, the two styles existed side by side, each being used as deemed appropriate by the composer.

In general, the Baroque period exhibits a number of stylistic traits that distinguish it from earlier periods. One of the major characteristics of Baroque music is a distinguished polarity between a treble voice (with treble meaning "pertaining to the highest voice) and an accompanying bass line (the lowest voice) that dictated the realization of harmonies. The style of the Renaissance evolved to place equal emphasis on all voices of a composition, voices that were entirely independent of each other. Seventeenth-century music, on the other hand, yielded a great amount of music written in homophonic textures, with the bass and treble voices being most prominent and inner voices simply "filling in" the harmony.

Another defining characteristic of the Baroque period was the development of a convention known as *basso continuo*. Italian for "continuous bass," composers wrote out melodies and a bass line, with the performers of the bass line left to fill in the appropriate harmonies according to figures indicated by the composer. While basso continuo became the standard practice in the Baroque, one should know that not every single piece called for basso continuo. As the role of basso continuo was accompaniment, it was obviously unnecessary for solo works for lute and keyboard instruments What is important to remember is that basso continuo refers not to a single performer, but rather a group of instrumentalists known as the *continuo group*. The number of players in the continuo group was rarely prescribed by the composer, was flexible, and could vary from composition to composition; however, the continuo group always consisted of specific types of instruments. A typical continuo group always consisted of at least one keyboard instrument (usually harpsichord, but sometimes with organ in cases of sacred music) and at least one bass stringed instrument, such as viola da gamba or cello. Additionally, the continuo group might include strummed instruments such as the lute or theorbo, or it might include a low-sounding wind instrument like the bassoon to reinforce the bass line.

The symbols indicated below the bass line were known as figured bass, a notational system that informed the performer of the harmonies that should be realized in a composition. The realization of these figures in performance led to a wide variety of interpretations, interpretations which varied based on the style of the piece and the particular tastes and skills of the player. Realization of figured bass was quite improvisatory in nature, as the performer had great latitude in their interpretation of the music. The basso continuo player might begin by playing only the bass line, then adding in a few chords based on the figured bass. Then the player might continue by doubling the treble voice, adding ornaments and embellishments as the player felt necessary.

Several other developments and practices marked the Baroque period as distinct from previous compositional styles. Composers in the seventeenth century frequently wrote music for both voices and instruments, each playing different parts. This is a significant departure from Renaissance music, in which instruments typically doubled the vocal parts (or played vocal music without any singers). This resulting practice became known as the *concertato medium,* which comes from the Italian *concertare,* "to reach agreement." The overriding concept is that a variety of contrasting voices and instruments are brought together harmoniously in a single musical work known as a *concerto.* Later in the seventeenth century and beyond, we will come to understand the concerto as a composition for soloist and orchestra, but in the early seventeenth century the meaning of concerto was much broader.

> ORNAMENTATION I LIKE.

The other two major hallmarks of Baroque music were the use of ornamentation and the shift from modal music to tonal music. Ornamentation, used sparingly (if at all) in the Renaissance became the norm in the Baroque. Aside from demonstrating a performer's individual style, ornaments or embellishments were frequently employed to aid in moving the affections. Ornaments occurred on a local level (such as trills added to a particular note), but they also occurred on a global level. For example, the *cadenza*— an extended elaborately-decorated passage demonstrating the virtuosity of the performer—was a common way of bringing a piece of music to a close. The church modes, which had long dominated the music of the Middle Ages and Renaissance, no longer characterized music. Instead, composers were writing in a harmonic language we now call *tonal music,* the system of writing in major and minor keys that are familiar with today. While some of the practices of the Baroque eventually felt out of fashion (such as basso continuo), others remain with us today, such as the development of tonality to replace modal music.

CHAPTER 12

CHAMBER AND CHURCH MUSIC IN THE SEVENTEENTH CENTURY

In the seventeenth century, music continued to serve very specific roles: secular music to be performed for social events, entertainment, the chamber, and theatre and sacred music to be performed in churches. Italy's role as a leader in musical innovation in Europe continued to flourish in the seventeenth century, both in chamber music and church music. While opera was the main focus of musical culture in Venice, the rest of Italy enjoyed a surge in secular music that was designed for small audiences. Music involved ensembles of voices and instruments for amateur musicians and the listening enjoyment of their peers. While strophic songs continued to be popular with the masses, the elite enjoyed vocal chamber music in a variety of forms and styles, many of which combined characteristics of madrigal, dance music, and dramatic music.

A survey of music history limits the ability to do justice to all forms of secular vocal music in the seventeenth century, so this chapter will focus on the three principal developments in song: concertato works, basso ostinato, and the cantata. In the previous chapter we learned that the concertato medium employed both voices and instruments playing individual parts. Italian composers churned out thousands of pieces for voice and accompanying basso continuo, sometimes with additional instruments. While many of the works were composed for one to three voices, some featured as many as six voices (and sometimes more!). Many of these songs were known much more widely than the operas of the time, and thus they became the music of the people.

The *concerted madrigal,* in particular, marks a major departure from the unaccompanied, polyphonic madrigal of the Renaissance. While styles ranged from imitative polyphony mirroring the sixteenth century to the *stile concitato* (the "excited style") of the seventeenth century, nearly all of these concerted madrigals employed a basso continuo. These madrigals were often set for one to three voices, but they occasionally called for additional instruments, resulting in instrumental introductions and ritornellos.

Of these concerted works, a number of them employed a technique called basso ostinato (also known as a **ground bass**). The **basso ostinato** was a compositional method where a short pattern in the bass would be repeated continuously over an ever-changing melody and harmony above it. The Italians don't get full credit for this one—the technique had already been in use for many years in the popular songs of Spain as well. Specific types of ground bass include the lament bass (a descending pattern of four notes known as a descending tetrachord) and the **chacona** (a lively dance-song form brought from Latin America to Spain and eventually to Italy). The descending tetrachord was called a lament bass because the pattern of falling pitches conveyed a sense of hopeless sorrow. The chacona (*ciaccona* in Italian), in contrast, was lively and upbeat.

Perhaps the most important genre of vocal music to emerge from the mid-seventeenth century was the **cantata,** which in Italian means "to be sung." Early in the century, the term would apply primarily to secular vocal works, accompanied by continuo and usually for solo voice, that were either lyrical or even dramatic in nature. Leading composers of secular cantatas in the mid-1600s included Antonio Cesti, Giacomo Carissimi, and Barbara Strozzi. Eventually the cantata will become a form of vocal music in the church as well, most notably in the church music of J. S. Bach.

KEEP IT GOIN', BOYS.

The continued independence of instruments from their vocal counterparts led to an increasing number of compositions intended solely for instrumental performance. Of course, the types and forms of instrumental music varied from nationality to nationality, but there are a number of types of compositions that were pervasive across Europe. Some of the most important forms of instrumental music of the mid-seventeenth century include the toccata, the ricercare and fugue, the keyboard fantasia, the sonata, and the chorale prelude.

The toccata of the Baroque did not vary much from the toccata of the late Renaissance except in terms of using tonal harmonies as opposed to using church modes. The *ricercare* and *fugue* were quite similar in the seventeenth century, both being very serious compositions based on a subject or theme that would be continuously developed and imitated throughout the course of the composition. While the ricercare will eventually fall out of fashion, the fugue will become an important staple of the late seventeenth and early eighteenth centuries and an inspiration for composers in the centuries to follow. The keyboard *fantasia,* an imitative work like the ricercare, had a much more complex formal organization than either the ricercare or toccata, and it was also much larger in scale and scope.

The *sonata* was a very broadly used term in the seventeenth century, referring to virtually any composition for instruments. From the Italian *sonare* "to be heard," sonatas of the seventeenth century often consisted of a work for one or two treble instruments plus basso continuo. Violins were the instrument of choice for sonatas of this time, and the sonata itself was usually composed to show off the particular nuances of the instrument for which it was composed. The other important instrumental composition in the early Baroque was the *chorale prelude,* an improvisational work for organ that was based on an existing chant or hymn tune. Both of

these terms (sonata and chorale prelude) will continue to be used to describe instrumental compositions for many years to come.

Alongside the developments in secular music, the church played a major role in the invention new forms and genres of sacred music. The *sacred concerto* was one of the leading genres of sacred music of the time, adopting a theatrical element to the setting of religious texts accompanied by basso continuo and incorporating elements of the concertato medium and operatic styles. The church sought a dramatic, effective means for communicating the message of the church through music, and the sacred concerto filled this role effectively and persuasively. The sacred concerto took both large-scale forms, written for multiple choirs and instruments, and small-scale forms, involving one or more soloists accompanied by organ and instrument or two. All sacred music of the time, including the sacred concerto, employed compositional styles of the Renaissance (now known as the *stile antico* or "old style") and more modern compositional styles (known as the *stile moderno*).

THESE ORATORIOS JUST SEEM TO WRITE THEMSELVES.

GIACOMO CARISSIMI

In seventeenth-century Rome a new genre of dramatic religious music emerged in the form of the **oratorio**. The name comes from the Italian word *oratorio*, which referred to a small prayer hall where the laity would gather to pray, listen to sermons, and sing devotional songs. The oratorio was revolutionary in that it combined elements of narrative, dialogue, and commentary, all in the form of music. At first this might seem similar to opera, which it was, but there were several important differences. One, the oratorio was always religious in nature. Two, the oratorio was seldom staged, if ever, and the action of the drama was never acted out as it was in opera. In the early Baroque, the leading composer of oratorio was Giacomo Carissimi (1605-1674), and the form would blossom in the late

Baroque in the compositions of G. F. Handel and in the Classical period in the music of Franz Joseph Haydn.

In the Lutheran church, Heinrich Schütz (1585-1672) proved to be the leading master of Italian styles. His output of sacred music included collections of psalm settings and other sacred songs, most notably his *Psalms of David* and *Cantiones sacrae*. Schütz also composed large-scale musical works, such as his large-scale concerto *Saul, was verfolgst du mich* for two choirs of voices and instruments, six vocal soloists, two violins, and basso continuo. A prominent genre in which Schütz composed was the *historia*, a musical composition based on a biblical story. He composed *historia* based on the Christmas story, as well as *The Seven Last Words of Christ*. The most popular and common type of *historia* was the **passion**, which recalled the suffering and death of Jesus' crucifixion. The passion will become an important genre in the music of later Baroque composers and again in the twentieth century.

Chapter 13

MUSIC OF THE WORLD IN THE SEVENTEENTH CENTURY

While form and genre has been the principle focus of the past several chapters, it is equally important to understand the significance of national style, particularly as we examine the middle and late Baroque period. Both culture and politics influenced national style, and while Italy remained the leading musical center, both France and England made significant contributions. In France, the king was the chief sponsor of music, often using it as a means to his own political ends through propaganda and social control. In contrast, the English monarchy had little influence on the development of music in England, which in turn led to public support for music and the invention of the public concert. French music was adopted by many areas of Germany, while Spain forged its own path. This chapter will focus primarily on the national styles of France and England, as well as the adoption of French styles in Italy.

Dance and the role of the arts in the monarchy were the central factors in the formation of a French Baroque style. King Louis XIV and his seven-decade reign (which began at the ripe young age of five!) greatly influenced French music and culture. Louis was constantly fixated on his ability to maintain power, and he used the arts as a means for disseminating his image as one of absolute power and authority. He considered himself the "Sun King," calling upon the ancient images of Apollo and symbolizing himself as the sole giver of light. He built expansive and opulent buildings, including a rebuilding of the Louvre (now an incredible museum) and the Palace at Versailles.

IT AIN'T ART UNLESS IT GLORIFIES ME— SO GO MAKE SOME!

LOUIS XIV

Dance, in particular, was an important component of both French culture and the court of King Louis. The *court ballet* was a distinctive, large-scale French genre of dance that was incredibly involved. An impressive musical-dramatic work, the court ballet was a multi-act composition that involved staging, scenery, choruses, professional dancers, and instrumental dancers, with members of the court assuming many of the roles. Court musicians numbered nearly 200 and involved a hierarchical organization like the state itself. Religious music was provided by the musicians of the Royal Chapel, which included singers, organists, and instrumentalists. The Music of the Chamber provided music for indoor entertainment, and consisted mostly of string, lute, flute, and harpsichord players. For outdoor events and ceremonies, such as those for the military, wind, brass, and percussion players of the Music of the Great Stable provided the music, sometimes in concert with the indoor musicians. French preference for the stringed instruments (namely the viol) eventually became the model for the modern *orchestra*—an instrumental ensemble with stringed instruments as the principal component.

By far, Louis XIV's favorite court musician was Jean-Baptiste Lully (1632-1687), who was in the king's employ for more than three decades. His success was largely in the composition of dramatic works (principally French opera), but he also composed music for religious services and ballets. One of the hallmarks of Lully's music was the *French overture,* which means "opening." It was the principal instrumental music used to open an opera or ballet, and its distinct style and form would

JEAN-BAPTISTE LULLY

become a topic for future music compositions. The French overture was marked by two distinct, repeated sections: the first was grand and majestic, homophonic and employing unequal rhythms that rushed to the downbeat; the second section was faster and usually imitative like a fugue.

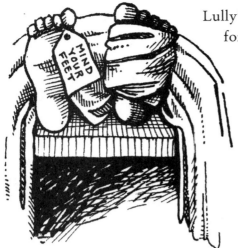

Lully's death quickly became legend for its unusual circumstances. In the Baroque period, conductors did not use a small wooden baton held in the hand to lead the ensemble; rather, they held a large staff which they pounded vertically against the ground to keep the pulse of the music. In a performance of one of his pieces, Lully accidentally struck his own foot, creating a wound that would not heal. Eventually, gangrene set in, and this infection led to Lully's death.

French dance music played an important role in music history as well in terms of form. French composers often grouped their dance music into *suites,* a collection of dances that each had their own distinct characteristics, chiefly in rhythm and tempo. Most of seventeenth-century dances were in binary form, meaning they consisted of two basically equal sections, each being repeated. The allemande, courante, sarabande, gigue, gavotte, and minuet were the principal dances in such a suite, and they would prove to be influential for later composers of instrumental suites in the Baroque.

Meanwhile across the channel, French-influenced and native genres of dramatic music grew in popularity in England. The English *masque* was a favorite of the court since the reign of King Henry VIII. While the masque shared many characteristics of opera, it was very different in that it was rarely composed by a single composer. In fact, the masque was much more similar to the French court ballet with its use of songs, dancing, choruses, instrumental music, scenery, and stage machinery.

HENRY PURCELL

While John Blow (1649-1708) and his pastoral masque *Venus and Adonis* were important to the development of the masque genre, Henry Purcell (1659-1695) was the leading composer and favorite son of the royal court and is best known for his dramatic music. His most well-known work is *Dido and Aeneas,* even though the three-act, four-role work can be performed in less than an hour. The overture and choruses are reminiscent of the dance rhythms of Lully, but he also incorporates Italian elements such as the *aria* or song, a rarity for French opera or English masque. The last *aria* or song of the work, *When I am laid in earth,* is a musical icon, composed over a descending tetrachord (lament bass) with terrifying dissonances meant to evoke a profound depth of sorrow.

Possibly more important than advances in musical composition was the invention of a social institution: the public concert. Until the 1670s, concerts were always performed in the privacy of a home or space of a patron, with invited audiences and performers employed by the patron. A growing middle class, a wealth of highly skilled musicians, and the monarchy's inability to afford paying musicians a decent wage resulted in an enterprise of public performances. This led to the building of commercial concert halls, with the trend spreading to major French and German cities by the middle of the eighteenth century.

CHAPTER 14

THE LATE BAROQUE PERIOD:

ITALY AND FRANCE

$\mathcal{C}$omposers of the late Baroque (ca. 1700-1750) were not inventing new styles, techniques, and genres for composition nearly as rapidly as composers had in the past; rather, they continued to build upon existing practices, often synthesizing them in new and creative ways. They continued to concern themselves with the doctrine of affections, basso continuo, the concertato medium, and genres of suite, concerto, sonata, cantata, and opera. This chapter focuses on the developments in the late Baroque in Italy and France, namely Vivaldi, Couperin, and Rameau, who were the leading composers in these regions.

Opera continued to reign in Italy as the most prestigious—and the most expensive—form of music, but growing in popularity was instrumental music. The concerto was perhaps the single most popular genre of instrumental music in the late Italian Baroque. Earlier we had examined the sacred concerto, but since that time the concerto evolved into the most important genre of Baroque instrumental music and established the orchestra as the most important instrumental ensemble. By 1700, composers were composing three different subtypes of concerto. The *orchestral concerto* did not involve soloists; rather, it focused on the contrast between the first violin part and the bass. The *concerto grosso* juxtaposed a small solo ensemble (called the *concertino*) against the full orchestra (called the concerto grosso). The *solo concerto* was similar to the concerto grosso with the exception that the ensemble of soloists was replaced by a single soloist, usually a violin. The concept of juxtaposing solo instruments against a full orchestra is an idea that dates back as far as Lully and his operas.

The most well-known composer in Italy was Venetian composer Antonio Vivaldi (1678-1741). Vivaldi spent most of his life and career in Venice as a virtuoso violinist, church musician, teacher, and composer. Vivaldi's principal employment was at the Pio Ospedale della Pietà. The Pietà was one of four orphanages for children who had either been orphaned or sent away because they were illegitimate. The orphanages were run like boarding schools, with the children receiving excellent educations, particularly in music under the tutelage of Vivaldi. It was at the Ospedale della Pietà that Vivaldi composed his well-known *Gloria in D major,* but it was his composition of instrumental works that drew the large audiences (and donations).

ANTONIO VIVALDI

I HAVE A LITTLE ANTIDOTE FOR SEASONAL AFFECTIVE DISORDER.

Vivaldi is remembered most for his numerous compositions of concertos, of which he wrote more than five hundred! While obviously each of the five hundred concertos was distinct from the rest, a running joke in the music world is that Vivaldi composed the same concerto five hundred times. In reality, Vivaldi's tuneful and fresh melodies, rhythmic excitement, and intimate knowledge of solo instruments are what make Vivaldi's concertos lasting works in music history. At the Pietà he had a host of skilled musicians at his disposal, and the demand for rapid output of new compositions precipitated the need for constantly creating fresh and creative works. His secret to success lay in a simple and flexible recipe for the concerto, in which he could change a few elements while leaving the essential form of the work intact. This formula has become known as the *ritornello form.*

At its most basic form, the ritornello form simply consisted of contrasting sections in the music between the full orchestra and the soloist. Each concerto would begin with the ritornello (remember, it is Italian for "refrain"), followed by a virtuosic *episode* played by the soloist with minimal accompaniment. The ritornello would then return (usually only partially), followed by another soloist episode. This alternating pattern would continue for the duration of the movement until finally concluding with a final statement of the full ritornello by the entire ensemble. Through tweaking this flexible form, Vivaldi was able to create a unique, fresh concerto each and every time. The best known concertos to this day are his *Four Seasons,* a set of four concertos—one for each season of the year and inspired by a poem he himself had written.

While Italy had musical centers in Rome, Naples, and Venice, Paris was the main hub of musical development in France. Careers in Paris were the ultimate dream for musicians, as success in Paris was the only path to true success and national acclaim. While other cities in France supported the musical arts, the most prestigious home of concert organizations was Paris; likewise, the majority of wealthy patrons and institutions resided in the French capital. The spread of Italian music and influence to Paris was welcomed by some and resisted by others, particularly by those who were leery of foreign influence.

A leading advocate of the blending of French and Italian musical styles was François Couperin (1668-1733). Couperin's career was indicative of the careers of many musicians: employment was needed in several places to make a living. Couperin served as organist to the king and as organist at the church of St. Gervais, but he earned the vast majority of his income as a private music teacher, instructing the aristocracy in harpsichord. Couperin also supplemented his income by publishing his compositions.

Couperin's synthesis of French and Italian styles is best seen in his chamber music. He unequivocally proclaimed in the preface of *Les gouts-réünis* that the perfect music would be a combination of the two styles: "The Italian and French styles have long divided up the Republic of Music in France. As for me, I have always esteemed the things that deserved to be, without regard to the composer or nation." He admired the music of both Lully and seventeenth-century Italian composer Arcangelo Corelli, and he honored them in two suites for two violins and harpsichord. The first he titled *The Apotheosis of Corelli;* the second he called *The Apotheosis of Lully.*

The other major player in French music in the Baroque was Jean-Philippe Rameau (1683-1764), a famed music theorist for the first forty years of his life, and later as a composer of chamber music and opera. As mentioned before, music in the Baroque shifted from the church modes that had long dominated compositions to a system of tonal music, the major and minor keys we know today. Rameau was one of the first music theorists to codify this new system of tonality through his writings, principally his *Treatise on Harmony* in 1722. Rameau's concepts, revolutionary at the time, are now the pillars of music theory today.

As a composer, Rameau established himself as the successor to Jean-Baptiste Lully. He instantly attracted a following after the premiere of his first opera, *Hippolyte et Articie,* followed by four more operas and opera-ballets in the next six years.

JEAN-PHILIPPE RAMEAU

His work, however, was not without controversy, and opera-goers fell into two sharply-divided camps: those who strongly supported Rameau and those who viewed his opera as an affront to Lully's legacy. While we now see change as a necessary element for progress and innovation, Lully loyalists heard Rameau's music as grotesque, difficult, and unnatural. By the 1750s, the controversy over Rameau's music subsided, and he was regarded as the most eminent living French composer and hailed as a champion of French music.

Chapter 15

THE LATE BAROQUE PERIOD:

J.S. BACH AND G.F. HANDEL

For the first time in European music history, German composers in the eighteenth century would be leaders in music, rivaling those of Italy, which had long set the bar for excellence in music. Telemann, Handel, members of the Bach family, Haydn, and Mozart all rise to prominence in the 1700s, creating new styles and genres and synthesizing those of the Italian, French, German, and other national traditions. While there were many prominent German composers of the late Baroque, this chapter will focus exclusively on J.S. Bach and G.F Handel, whose music has endured for centuries and serve as the example against which many other composers (and their works) are measured.

Music history has proven Johann Sebastian Bach (1685-1750) to be the consummate musician and composer, possibly the greatest of all composers of all time. While he is revered today for his compositions, his renown in Protestant Germany was due to his skill as an organist and choirmaster (although his compositions were admired in his day). Bach spent most of his life working as a Lutheran church musician, spending time and holding posts in the cities of Arnstadt, Mühlhausen, Weimar, and Leipzig. All of his positions required weekly composition of new musical works and the preparation of singers and instrumentalists alike. While Bach held a number of important posts in his career, the concept of a freelance musician was not as we think of it today.

For example, when he requested that the duke of Weimar release him from his position to accept another job, the duke had him imprisoned for a month before finally releasing him! In Leipzig, he was required to make a pledge of allegiance to the town and to swear to lead an exemplary life—in fact, he was not even allowed to leave the town without the mayor's permission.

Bach's output as a composer is one of the greatest magnitude, having composed hundreds of works in a wide variety of genres and styles. As a church organist, Bach's works focused primarily on music to accompany a Lutheran church service: he composed a host of toccatas, preludes,

AND IN MY SPARE TIME I FATHERED 20 CHILDREN— WHEW...

fugues, and chorale settings. In all, he composed more than two hundred settings of chorales. While working in Weimar, he compiled another forty-five short chorale preludes into a single manuscript known as the *Orgelbüchlein* (Little Organ Book). These chorale preludes served to introduce the hymn that the congregation would sing immediately after. While these works were exclusively German in nature, Bach also composed organ pieces that were influenced by Vivaldi. He arranged several of Vivaldi's concertos so that they could be played on organ, and stylistic elements of Vivaldi's concertos can be heard in Bach's preludes and fugues.

In addition to composing for organ, Bach also wrote a host of works for the harpsichord, again including preludes, fugues, fantasias, toccatas, and suites. His harpsichord suites demonstrate his cosmopolitan approach to composition: he wrote several suites in English and French styles, and they have been grouped and named posthumously *English Suites* and *French Suites.* He incorporated Italian styles in his *Italian Concerto* for keyboard. Of his keyboard works, the two-volume *Well-Tempered Clavier* is perhaps his most famous. Each of the volumes contains twenty-four pairs of preludes and fugues, one for each of the twelve major and twelve minor keys. The development of equal temperament made this a novel concept for keyboard music. While each of the pieces in the *WTC* were works of art in their own right, they also served as pedagogical models for composing in specific styles.

Of Bach's orchestral compositions, the six *Bran-denburg Concertos* are his best known. The works were dedicated in 1721 to the Margrave of Brandenburg who had requested some compositions from Bach, although the music had been composed previously within the past ten years or so. On the other end of the instrumental music spectrum, Bach also excelled in the composition of chamber music. He composed fifteen sonatas for solo instruments and harpsichord; six sonatas for violin alone; and six suites for cello alone. Although not unheard of at the time, his compositions for solo instruments without any accompaniment were indeed a novelty at the time.

In 1700 the term *cantata*, previously a secular work, took on a new form. Lutheran theologian and poet Erdmann Neumeister conceived of a new type of sacred work that not only incorporated the standard biblical, liturgical, and chorale texts, but also interpolated poetic texts to further emphasize the message of the day's Gospel reading. The new Lutheran cantata incorporated a host of great past traditions into one work: the chorale, the solo song, operatic elements, and the concertato medium. The church cantata was at the center of the Lutheran liturgy in Leipzig, both at the St. Nicholas and St. Thomas churches (yes, Bach had two church jobs at the same time). The works typically opened with a choral movement[5], alternated with *recitatives* (free, speech-like declamations of text) and arias, and concluding with a four-part harmonized chorale.

The Leipzig churches were incredibly demanding: they required fifty-eight cantatas for each of the three church years (scriptures for the church rotated in three-year cycles), in addition to music for other

---

[5] It is important to note that choral or chorale movements were usually sung by one voice on each part. While there was a trained choir that sung in the services, the cantatas were performed by vocal soloists and were not likely sung by choirs as they are today.

liturgical and festival services. While Bach wrote many more than this, approximately two hundred of his cantatas were preserved for posterity. How did Bach manage to write so much music every week, with each cantata ranging in duration between fifteen and thirty minutes each? One way that Bach saved himself some time was by reworking or adapting musical material that he had previously composed, although this still left him an immense amount of work each week. In addition to the church canta- tas, Bach also composed large-scale works for Good Friday in the form of passions. The two surviving passions are pillars of choral-orchestral music today: the *St. John Passion* and the *St. Matthew Passion*. Both works incorporate recita-

tives, arias, chorales, choruses, and orchestral accompaniment, but the *St. Matthew Passion* is unique in that the work is composed for double cho- rus and double orchestra. Bach's *opus magnum* is his *Mass in B Minor*, a collection of Catholic Mass Ordinary movements composed at different times in his life that he carefully preserved together as a gift for posterity. Due to its unprecedented length, scope, and intricacy, it is unlikely that the mass was ever performed as a singular work in Bach's lifetime.

While Bach's influence and status as the greatest composer of the Baroque and quite possibly all time, George Frideric Handel (1685- 1759) comes in at a close second. Like Bach, Handel was a cosmopoli- tan figure: he was a native German, he composed Italian opera, and he resided in England, where he composed English oratorio and set the precedent for the genre. For thirty-six years of his life, he dedicated himself to the composition of opera, the mastery of which was the am- bition of most composers of his time. His *Rinaldo* was the first Italian opera composed for London, and his *Giulio Cesare* (Julius Caesar) is hailed as one of his greatest achievements in opera.

Handel's operas are staples in the canon of Baroque opera, but his work as a composer of oratorio is what ensured his place in music history. Similar to earlier oratorios, Handel's oratorios were sacred in subject and presented in concert in a religious building instead of on stage. The English oratorio was unstaged and did not employ the scenery, acting, and stage machinery of opera. His most significant innovation in the genre was his use of chorus, an element he borrowed from Italian opera. The choruses—sung by actual choirs of vocalists, not soloists—served as structural pillars of the oratorio, as well as providing important commentary on the preceding music.

IT MAY NOT BE GOSPEL BUT IT'S MORE FUN TO SING.

GEORGE FRIDERIC HANDEL

Handel's oratorios covered a host of biblical stories, including *Israel in Egypt, Esther,* and *Saul,* but by and large his most popular and successful oratorio was *Messiah,* a work that continues to be performed regularly throughout the world today. He composed the oratorio in a mere fourteen days for a performance in Dublin, Ireland, in 1742. The oratorio, which in three parts retells the story of Jesus's birth, life, passion, and resurrection through both Old and New Testament scriptures, was performed annually in London as a charity event for the Foundling Hospital. Like Bach's passions, Handel's oratorios incorporate a wide variety of musical forms including arias, recitatives, choruses, and orchestral accompaniment. Handel's work in the genre of oratorio would prove to be an inspiration for the oratorios of later composers such as Haydn and Mendelssohn.

FINALLY!
CLASSICAL
"CLASSICAL MUSIC"

Chapter 16

CLASSICAL MUSIC AND CLASSICAL STYLE

In the late eighteenth century, we see the development of a new idiom known as the classical style, among many other names. Ambiguously, the term "classical" can refer broadly to all art music of all periods composed in the vein that we have studied thus far (and will continue to examine in the remaining chapters). More narrowly it can be used to describe specifically the style of the late eighteenth century. This ambiguity is not without reason: in the nineteenth century, the music of Bach, Handel, Haydn, Mozart, and Beethoven were considered the classics of music, much like the classics of literature and art, and their music formed the core of classical repertoire. Later in the nineteenth and twentieth centuries, that term grew to encompass all art music composed. The term "Baroque" then became the term used to describe the music of Bach and Handel, with "classical" left to describe that of the late eighteenth century. This is how one can say that not all classical music is classical!

Returning to the classical style itself, another common name for the style that developed in the late eighteenth century was *galant*, a French term that began as a description for the courtly manner of literature and soon became used to describe anything and everything that was modern, chic, sophisticated, and in style.

Juxtaposed against the learned or strict style of writing (which later we would call Baroque), the galant style was freer, more song-like, and with short-breathed, repeated gestures. The galant style also placed unprecedented emphasis on the tunefulness and importance of the melody, which was accompanied by simple harmonies.

Another term similar to the galant style was the *empfindsamer Stil* (German for "sentimental style"), known generally as the **empfindsam style.** Given its etymological roots, it's no wonder that the term is associated primarily with German music; music marked by surprising turns in harmony, anxious rhythmic activity, and free, speech-like melody. Despite its German name and application, the empfindsam style—like the galant style—originated in the description of Italian music. Regardless of the terminology used, the classical style took its shape from the influence of vocal music, and this classical style will soon apply to instrumental works, creating a new approach to melody and form. What is important to remember is that the Baroque style did not suddenly fall out of fashion on the first day of 1750; rather, the Baroque and the Classical styles overlapped for a number of years, nearly until the turn of the century.

In the Classical period, composers still concerned themselves with the affections. A new ideology in the field of human psychology led to innovations in the emotional qualities of music. Those who studied human psychology believed that that once a person experiences or rouses a particular emotion, he or she would remain under the influence of that affect until moved to a different affect. In the Baroque period, composers aimed to evoke a single affect for a single movement or section of music. In contrast, composers in the Classical period realized that the emotional state was fluid, and thus a single movement of music could evoke a variety of emotions. This is what paved the way for unexpected turns in the character of music in the Classical period.

Chapter 17

INSTRUMENTAL MUSIC TAKES THE STAGE (AGAIN)

Instrumental music in the Classical period was affected by the new musical idiom and other developments of the time. The new emphasis on vocal music which precipitated the new classical style extended its influence to instrumental music as well. Regularity of phrasing; tuneful melodies; contrasting emotions, textures, and styles; and hints of drama all found their way into instrumental music. Oddly enough, instrumental music gained further independence and importance by borrowing these styles and ideals from the very vocal music it was distinguishing itself from.

The most significant development in instruments themselves was the invention of the pianoforte, known colloquially as the piano.

The harpsichord (and its cousin the clavichord) had long been the standard, but due to the rising popularity of the piano, they eventually fell out of fashion. As described earlier, the piano sounds by a hammer that strikes each string and then falls away, while the strings of a harpsichord are plucked and the strings of a clavichord struck by tangents that remain touching the string until the key is no longer depressed. This advance in keyboard technology allowed for a player to play more expressively through touch alone, creating contrast in volume and articulation; because the strings were plucked, the harpsichord lacked these expressive possibilities.

Chamber music began to focus on small groups of stringed instruments numbering two to five, with the *string quartet* (comprised of two violins, one viola, and one cello) the most common and popular. A new instrument also was born around 1710 and became a staple of the woodwind family by 1780: the clarinet. The clarinet joined a family of woodwinds that already included the flute, oboe, and bassoon. By the middle of the century, the clarinet was already a common instrument in the orchestra.

Keyboard music was one of the most popular genres among composers, performers, and listeners alike in the late eighteenth century. The popular forms and genres of the Baroque (such as the prelude, fugue, toccata, and dance suite) faded away and made room for the *sonata,* a new genre of music using an old term that describes a work for solo instrument in three or four contrasting movements. The keyboard sonata was one popular genre, but there were a number of sonatas composed for solo instrument plus keyboard. Even though the sonata has assumed an old name, the content of the music was new: the galant style.

The first movement of a sonata followed a specific form called first-movement form, or more commonly **sonata form.** Important to keep in mind is that sonata form did not just occur in sonatas; rather, this first-movement form was a common form for a variety of genres! A simplified explanation of the form describes it as a three-part form. The first part, called the **exposition,** presents two different themes or theme groups. The second part, called the **development,** does just that: it takes musical material from the exposition and reworks it in new aspects or combinations while unstably wandering through a variety of keys. The **recapitulation,** as its name suggests, is the third and final part where the material from the exposition returns and bring the work to a close.

I DO LOVE THE KEYBOARD.

DOMENICO SCARLATTI

Two of the most important composers of keyboard music in the mid-1700s were Domenico Scarlatti and C.P.E. Bach. Scarlatti (1685-1757) was hardly known in Europe during his lifetime, but his keyboard music demonstrates an unparalleled creativity for the time. He was the son of Alessandro Scarlatti and a contemporary of Handel, and he served in various courts outside of Italy, including those in Portugal and Spain. Scarlatti composed more than 550 keyboard sonatas, and his use of the two-part binary form led to the eventual development of the sonata form (he often brought back the music from the first part of his binary at the end of the second part).

Carl Philip Emanuel Bach (1714-1788), the son of J.S. Bach, was one of the most influential composers of his generation. He served the court of Frederick the Great in Berlin for nearly 30 years before becoming the music director of the five main churches in Hamburg. C.P.E. Bach composed in a host of genres, including oratorios, songs, concertos, and chamber music, but his most significant contributions were in works for keyboard. Unlike the music of Scarlatti, Bach's music focused on melody, unexpected harmonies, and building suspense, a clear implementation of the empfindsam style. Additionally, his use of the fast-slow-fast organization for three-movement keyboard works set the standard for future sonatas.

AH, I'M JUST A CHIP OFF THE OLD BACH.

CARL PHILIP EMANUEL BACH

In addition to the growth of keyboard music, the orchestra experienced a surge in popularity during the eighteenth century, resulting in the development of the symphony, the major orchestral genre of the time. The Classical *symphony* can be described as an orchestral work of three or four movements in which all members of the ensemble play together without a separation between soloist and the orchestra, thus distinguishing it from the concerto. By the end of the century, the symphony would be considered the pinnacle of instrumental music.

The symphony was descendent of more than one instrumental genre, although it takes its name from the Italian *sinfonia* (opera overture). These opera overtures had no connection to any of the music to follow in the opera, and they often took the form of fast-slow-fast. Orchestral concertos also tended to follow the fast-slow-fast structure for their three movements, and the church sonatas in northern Italy followed this model as well. All of these similarities point to multiple influences in the development of the symphony.

By the end of the eighteenth century, instruments were singing! Composers took the new galant style that they learned from and applied to vocal music, and they imposed it upon their instrumental compositions, giving instrumental music independence and more "street cred" in its own right. The development of new genres, such as the piano sonata, string quartet, and symphony, became the foundation of instrumental music, and the new pieces created in these genres gained wide popularity among the middle- and upper-class amateurs and concertgoers.

Chapter 18

MOZART, HAYDN, AND QUINTESSENTIAL "CLASSICAL" COMPOSITION

he career of a professional musician in the late eighteenth century took on a new form, as many made money through teaching, public performance, and commissions for new compositions, in addition to the tried and true patronage of royalty, churches, and municipalities. Composers also faced a new challenge: in addition to pleasing their patrons, demand for entertaining music for the public increased greatly, influencing composers in an attempt to satisfy both constituencies.

The masters of achieving broad popular appeal were Joseph Haydn (1732-1809) and Wolfgang Amadeus Mozart (1756-1791), and their music has come to serve as the quintessence of the Classical period. Aside from their exceptional careers and compositions, both composers demonstrated a unique ability to appeal to audiences in a lasting and meaningful way through their synthesis of styles and traditions. Haydn built his acclaim by working under the patronage of the Prince of Esterházy, while Mozart gained fame immediately as a child prodigy, touring Europe as a performer and composing before he reached double digits in age.

WOLFGANG AMADEUS MOZART

SPARE THE BATON AND SPOIL THE COMPOSER I ALWAYS SAY.

Most of Haydn's career was spent in service to the Esterházy family, the most powerful noble family in Hungary known for their generosity and patronage of music. Haydn's job: to compose whatever music the prince demanded. He also conducted performances, maintained the repair of musical instruments, and oversaw the training and supervision of all of the estate's musicians. Although the Esterházy court was geographically isolated, it proved an ideal environment for the developing composer, where he composed a range of music from orchestral works to operas to masses. Although Haydn's contract specifically prohibited the selling or dissemination of any of his compositions, black market copies of his works eventually found their way across Europe, thus spreading his fame and reputation across the continent. In 1790, Haydn was eventually given a pension and released from his court position; he moved to Vienna, but took two extended trips to London, where he conducted concerts, taught students from noble families, and composed a number of new works.

HMMM, I'LL FINISH THE LONDON SYMPHONIES THEN I'LL WRITE ANOTHER THANK YOU NOTE TO THE ESTERHÁZY'S.

JOSEPH HAYDN

Haydn has been referred to as the "father of the symphony" because of his symphonies' broad appeal, high quality, and wide dissemination (not because he invented the genre, which we have already learned he didn't!). Haydn's symphonies were staples of the classical repertory of the nineteenth century; a concert wouldn't be complete without one. Haydn's symphonies are marked by a four-movement structure: a fast movement in sonata form; a slow movement; a minuet and trio (dance movements commonly paired together); and a fast finale. While visiting London, he composed his now exalted *London* Symphonies, twelve symphonic works that are the crowning achievement of his compositional career. In these symphonies, Haydn took his own compositions to new heights, with daring harmonies, memorable melodies, and intense rhythms.

Haydn also has been called the "father of the string quartet," perhaps for better reason than the "father of the symphony." Although he was not the first composer to conceive of the genre, he certainly was one of the earliest composers and set a high bar for the mastery of the composition. Unlike the symphony, which was usually performed by professional musicians in a public venue, the string quartet was usually played by amateur musicians for their own enjoyment (let us be clear: "amateur" does not mean lacking skill). As such, Haydn's string quartets seem to be composed directly for the players and not an audience; the works often feature an interplay or dialogue among the four string instruments. One of his quartets earned the moniker *The Joke*, because of Haydn's witty, almost comical approach to its composition. In one of the movements, he inserts long, uncomfortable pauses that interrupt the "thought" of the theme. These unexpected pauses are funny because they make both players and listeners aware of their own expectations for the music.

Haydn enjoyed success not only in the composition of instrumental works, but also in his creation of vocal compositions. He composed a number of large-scale, festive masses while serving the Esterházy family, and his last six masses exemplify the height of drama, each featuring four solo vocalists, chorus, and full orchestra with trumpets and timpani.

Haydn blended traditional elements like fugal writing with drama and, of course, the galant style. Inspired by a performance of Handel's *Messiah*, Haydn burst into tears and proclaimed of Handel, "He is the master of us all." This inspiration led to the composition of his *The Creation*, based on texts adapted from the Book of Genesis and Milton's *Paradise Lost*. The work is revolutionary in a number of ways: Haydn takes text depiction to new depths (such as the contrabassoon depicting the roaring lion); he builds on Handel's use of chorus, where the choir is the heavenly host proclaiming God's glory at the end of each; and he publishes the oratorio in both German and English, the first bilingual libretto in history.

Haydn was intimately familiar with the music of Mozart; they admired each other and considered each other a friend; however, they led drastically different lives. Haydn was content spending several decades in the service of a single family, while Mozart spent the majority of his short life as a freelance musician in Vienna. Haydn's fame and reputation grew over the course of his life, while Mozart's career began when he was but a young child, perhaps fortuitously in light of his early death. Despite these inherent differences, the two composers eventually came to represent the quintessence of the music of their time.

Mozart was born into a musical family: his father Leopold was an accomplished violinist and composer, and he exposed his children to a wide range of musical genres and styles at a very young age. At the young age of six, Mozart was already touring Europe with his family. Mozart's career would look much like the musical tours of his youth, taking him to Milan, Salzburg, and Vienna. He earned money from various posts under the patronage of an aristocrat or institution and by freelancing as a performer, teacher, and composer.

As a virtuoso pianist, it is no wonder that he composed a wealth of repertoire for the piano, including sonatas, fantasias, variations, and piano duets (for two players at one piano). His nineteen piano sonatas have become staples of pedagogical repertoire, and they were exceedingly popular at the time as well. His sonatas are marked by songlike melodies in the right hand accompanied by a simple harmonic figure in the left hand, as well as his blending of various styles and emotions. Mozart also composed a number of string quartets, although not nearly as prolifically as Haydn did. In fact, Mozart emulated Haydn's compositional prowess in the genre in his six *Haydn* Quartets, although he did so in his own musical language and style.

Like Haydn, Mozart composed many symphonies (more than fifty), but by far his greatest success was in the composition of opera. Mozart operas have become regular features in opera houses around the world. *The Marriage of Figaro, Don Giovanni,* and *Così fan tutte* (Thus Do All Women) were and still are immensely successful as comic opera, as are his serious operas *La clemenza di Tito* (The Mercy of Titus) and *The Magic Flute. The Magic Flute* is especially important in the history of opera: composed in German (its German title is *Die Zauberflöte*), the rich and profound music of the opera ranks it as the first great German opera.

The Magic Flute was one of Mozart's last completed compositions before his untimely death, preventing him from completing his renowned **Requiem.** His unfinished *Requiem* has long been shrouded in mystery and legend. While there remain many unanswered questions about the *Requiem,* there is much that we do know about the work that has transcended time and permeated popular culture. For example, when Mozart accepted the anonymous commission, he hardly could have foreseen his own untimely death, as he had several other major compositions in the works. We also know that his wife Constanze contracted several other composers (Franz Jakob Freystädtler, Josef Eybler, and ultimately Franz Süssmayr) to finish the work so she could collect the rest of the commission fee. Based on the extant autograph score and notes of the *Requiem*, we know what music is purely Mozart and what has been either completed or newly composed by others.

At the time of his death, Mozart had completed the Introit in its entirety (including complete music for the orchestra) and with the exception of the Lacrimosa, of which only eight measures were written, he fully composed the four vocal parts and bass line from the Kyrie through the end of the Offertory. Using fragments of musical material, Süssmayr completed the orchestra parts for the Kyrie, Sequence, and Offertory, and he composed entirely new music for the Sanctus, Benedictus, and Agnus Dei. Süssmayr also completed the work (the Communion) with a return of the music from the first two movements, which he believed was Mozart's intention.

FRANZ SÜSSMAYR

WHAT WOULD MOZART WRITE?

Since the end of the eighteenth century, Haydn and Mozart have been hailed as the greatest of the classical composers. Although they followed very different career paths, each found great success as composers and performers, and their compositions endured for centuries after their deaths. Their works provided models upon which Beethoven and composers of the nineteenth century would base their own compositions, and their music would ultimately become known as "classical," forming the core of the Western art music repertory.

Chapter 19

BEETHOVEN:
TO BE CLASSICAL OR
ROMANTIC, THAT IS
THE QUESTION

The end of the eighteenth century and beginning of the nineteenth century was a time of tumult, of revolution. Between 1799 and 1804, Napoleon Bonaparte, a decorated general and war hero in the French army, decided to ignore the elected legislature, consolidate military power, and crown himself emperor. The French revolution led to the Napoleonic wars, with Napoleon invading neighboring states, expanding French territories, installing his siblings as rulers in other states, and bringing an end to the 840-year-old Holy Roman Empire. While the French Revolution and Napoleonic wars ultimately failed after his loss at Waterloo and then exile, they helped unify national identities as determined by heritage and culture, not by the monarch persons were subject to.

Meanwhile, another less violent revolution was taking place: the Industrial Revolution. The technological advances in the Industrial Revolution shifted economies from agrarian to manufacturing-based. Innovations in technology led to machines that enabled large factories to mass produce items, thus lowering prices and increasing production. The Industrial Revolution indeed was a boon for many economies, as it resulted in new-found prosperity for much of the population.

Ludwig van Beethoven (1770-1827) and his music embody the ideas of revolution, and his music accurately reflects the tumult that plagued Europe in his day. The title of this chapter asks a question: Is the music of Beethoven classical or romantic in style? The simple, yet not-so-simple, answer is yes. Just by looking at Beethoven's dates, we can see that his life spans two different sections and two different stylistic periods. Beethoven absorbed the styles of Haydn and Mozart, yet progressively throughout his life, he led a revolution of his own that would change the sound of music forever.

THREE INTENSE PERIODS.

Although seemingly simplistic, Beethoven's career and music can be divided into three periods, divisions made by a scholar shortly after Beethoven's death that are still applied to this day. The first period starts with his birth in 1770 and ends about

100

LUDWIG VAN BEETHOVEN

THERE USED TO BE MUSIC IN THIS HORN.

1802, a year of crisis when Beethoven realized his gradual loss of hearing. During this time, Beethoven mastered the musical language of his forbearers (Haydn and Mozart), yet also found his own personal musical language. The second period lasts through about the end of 1814, another critical year for Beethoven in which his hearing was nearly gone, and he began to suffer from family troubles and growing isolation. In this period, his popularity grew immensely, as he raised music to a new level of expression and drama. His third and final period lasted from 1815 until his death in 1827. In this last stage of his life and career, Beethoven's musical works became more introspective, more difficult for performers to play, and more difficult for audiences to understand.

The first period of Beethoven's life can be divided into two parts, based on geography: his youth spent in Bonn and his first ten years in Vienna. He began his musical studies at a young age under the tutelage of his father and other local musicians; at the age of twenty-two, he made the five-hundred-mile stagecoach trip to Vienna in 1792 so that he could study with a true master: Joseph Haydn. Although Haydn left Vienna to visit London only two years later, Beethoven continued his studies and began to establish himself quickly as a skilled pianist and composer. With the generosity of several wealthy patrons, Beethoven gave a number of public performances that kickstarted his career.

Because Beethoven was a piano virtuoso, it is no surprise that piano works would be among his first compositions. Among other genres, his piano sonatas were incredibly popular with the amateur market, the traditional target audience for solo keyboard works, but even his earliest sonatas increased the technical demands on the performer. Beethoven followed the galant tradition established by Mozart, using strong contrasts in style or emotion to delineate structure and explore a broad expressive spectrum. Because he knew that Haydn was the preeminent composer of string quartets, Beethoven waited until he had established himself in Vienna before trying his hand at the genre. He knew that his string quartets would immediately be compared to those of Haydn, but he accepted it as an opportunity to prove himself as a superior composer.

Beethoven's middle period, beginning around 1803, was marked by compositions in a new, more ambitious style. His immense popularity, established reputation, and wide support from patrons and publishers freed him to take more risks his in compositions. Because he was in a strong financial state, Beethoven was able to be deliberate in writing his compositions, often revising and polishing his works many times before finally completing them. At the same time, he was dealing with his own personal crisis: the realization that his growing hearing loss was permanent, something inconceivable for an artist whose medium was sound. After a brief contemplation of suicide, Beethoven found an inner resolve to continue composing, and his personal courage is reflected in the music of this period. His musical themes seem to tell a narrative of a hero who, after many struggles and difficulties, ultimately emerges triumphant. This type of dramatic narrative in instrumental music was indeed a new concept in music history.

While Beethoven continued to develop his musical themes and material in the manner of Haydn, he expanded forms to an unprecedented scale. One work that epitomizes Beethoven's new approach is his third symphony, the *Eroica* Symphony (Heroic Symphony, a title he coined himself). The symphony was revolutionary in two primary ways. First, the symphony was markedly longer and more expansive than any other symphony ever composed. Second, the title of the symphony and its musical content suggest a dramatic narrative, one where a hero is celebrated and expresses the greatness of that hero. In many ways, the piece is a reflection of Beethoven's own personal struggles and his ability to overcome in spite of mounting odds against him. Other important works in this period include his opera *Fidelio*, three piano concertos, and his fifth and sixth symphonies (Symphony No. 5 is perhaps one of the most recognizable compositions in history).

NAH, THAT'S DUMB, DA, DUMB, DUMB.

Beethoven's late period is one marked by increased personal depression, greater isolation, and slowed output of compositions. Beethoven's deafness continued to worsen, and by 1818, he realized that he lost his hearing nearly entirely. Because of this, he lost contact with friends and family, retreated into his own mind, and suffered from family problems, poor health, and paranoid fears about his finances. His music reflected these major life and psychological shifts. Instead of composing for popular appeal, Beethoven directed his music at the true scholars and connoisseurs of music. Classical forms remained the foundation of his music, yet they were covered in layers of early romantic ideals and dramatic expression.

Beethoven's music continued to expand in scope, and at the same time his compositions grew increasingly cerebral. His works are characterized by an emphasis on unity within works, employment of imitation (namely, fugue), and use of traditional styles as a reflection on those styles. Beethoven's approach to composition in his late period can best be summarized in his *String Quartet in C# minor, Op. 131*[6]. The quartet was expanded to seven movements (in comparison to the traditional four-movement string quartet), to be played without interruption or pause. Unlike the typical fast movement that begins a string quartet, Beethoven begins the first movement of *Op. 131* with a slow-breathed, melancholy fugue. Beethoven's last public performances before his death were of the iconic *Missa Solemnis* (Solemn Mass) and Symphony No. 9, two works of unprecedented of scope, length, breadth, and depth.

---

[6] *This string quartet serves as the connecting theme and main focus of the movie* A Late Quartet *(2012).*

IT'S NOT ALL LOVEY-DOVEY: THE ROMANTIC PERIOD

Chapter 20

WHAT IS ROMANTICISM ANYWAY?

*M*usic in the Romantic period (roughly 1820 through the end of the century) paralleled Romanticism in literature and art; it was marked by increased emphasis on melody, individuality, novelty, and emotion. Derived from the medieval romance, a poem or story about a heroic person or event, the word *Romantic* was associated with ideals outside of the everyday reality, such as things that were legendary, distant, or fantastic. The term started as a descriptor for the literature and art of the nineteenth century and was eventually applied to music of the time. Romantic music focused on expression of one's self and on the identity of the individual; furthermore, it sought to be original, extreme, provocative, interesting, and expressive. By contrast, music of the Classical period was marked by elegance, restraint, simplicity, and universal appeal. In this light, it is apparent that Beethoven indeed was the bridge between the two periods, for his compositions reflected the ideals of both periods.

Composers in the Romantic idiom sought to write music that would appeal to the amateur performers and audience, and they achieved this through offering something new and individual that made their compositions stand out in a crowd of music. They aimed to write memorable and tuneful melodies, interesting accompaniments, strong musical and extra-musical imagery, national and exotic styles, and evocative and exciting titles. Competition for sales of published music led to increasing innovations in harmony and tonality. As an art form, Romantic music placed great value on beautiful melodies and captivating harmonies within small forms such as short piano pieces and songs, although this ideal eventually translated into larger forms as well.

Romanticism was a direct reaction to the culture and society of Europe at that time. Science and technology were the driving force in societies and their economies, and Romanticism sought to escape this mundane reality to places that were mythical, dreamlike, or supernatural. As people began moving away from the countryside and into large municipalities, Romanticism embraced rural life and sought refuge and inspiration in Mother Nature. The Industrial Revolution

You SUPPOSE IT'S OUR FAULT?

brought about mass production and uniformity; Romantics regarded highly the individual, novelty, boundlessness, and the exotic. Art was no longer simply a means for making a living; it was a way to escape the realities of life and access a "higher realm."

With these dramatic shifts in musical aesthetics, composers felt the freedom and desire to express an even wider and more intense range of emotions. While composers of the Romantic period showed deference to the traditional forms, the Romantic aesthetic pushed them to break the bonds of traditional form and explore new ideas in music. In some respects, instrumental music was the most ideal Romantic art form, as it was free from the limitations and concreteness of words and images, thus being able to express more than words themselves. Such instrumental works were considered *absolute music,* free from any associated words or images. Romantic composers also wrote *characteristic music* (a piece that suggests a mood, personality or scene that is usually suggested by the title) and *programmatic music,* a work that specifically recounts a particular narrative or tale, often delineated in an accompanying text called a program.

This brief description of the development and aesthetic ideals of the Romantic period will help you better understand the music (and context) of Romantic composers in the next four chapters.

Chapter 21

INNOVATION IN VOCAL AND PIANO MUSIC

The trends described in the previous chapter are reflected best in the songs of the Romantic era. Songs were composed mostly for voice and piano (either played by the singer or accompanied by a pianist), as the medium required minimal forces while offering a wide range of expressive possibilities. Songs varied in form and length, from short, simple, strophic settings of a melody (the melody and simple accompaniment repeating with each stanza of text) to miniature dramas that unfold throughout the piece, with stark contrasts in style and even the inclusion of multiple characters sung by one singer. The most important and esteemed form of song was the German *lied* (German for "song"). In many ways, it was the ideal Romantic art form, combining elements of poetry, music, expression, musical imagery, and even aspects of folk style.

After about 1800, the popularity of the lied soared, with publication of German song collections increasing one hundred-fold between the late 1700s to the early 1800s. Poetry, the main source of text for the lied, drew upon both classical and folk traditions and frequently emphasized themes of the human experience and the individual versus greater forces, such as nature or society. The lyric, modeled after the great lyric poets of ancient Greece and Rome, was the primary genre of poetry. A short, strophic poem, it focused on a single subject that expressed a personal sentiment or perspective. Another common poetic form was the ballad, an imitation of the folk ballads of Britain. Ballads told a story, often alternating narrative and dialogue and dealing with some supernatural incident or fantastic adventure. Composers of lieder (the plural of *lied*) often grouped their songs together in *song cycles,* where each song was meant to be performed immediately after the preceding song like a multimovement work.

The masters of the lied were, not surprisingly, German composers, chiefly Franz Schubert and Robert Schumann. Schubert (1797-1828) was the first great composer of the Romantic lied and was prolific in many other genres as well. Like Mozart, he died at an early age (thirty-one after suffering from syphilis) but produced an incredible body of music that has withstood the test of time. In his short career, he composed more than six hundred songs, thirty-five pieces for chamber ensembles, twenty-two piano sonatas, many short piano pieces, seventeen large-scale dramatic works, six masses, and about 200 other choral works. One can hardly imagine the music that would have come from the mind of Schubert had he lived a normal lifespan!

Although Schubert set the poetry of many writers, one of his favorite sources of text was the poetry of Goethe, whose poetry served for nearly sixty song settings. For Schubert, the music and the text were absolute equals; the music did not serve as a framework for the text, nor did the text merely serve as an inspiration for the music. Schubert desired to fully embody the characters, atmosphere, situation, and emotions of the poetry through elements of melody, harmony, form, and accompaniment. In some instances, he set poems in a *modified strophic form,* in which Schubert repeats music for some of the stanzas, but makes changes or uses new music for others. His melodies aimed to perfectly reflect the character, mood, and situation of poem, and his accompaniments did as well. The piano accompaniments ranged from simple harmonic realizations to dramatic depictions of the scene, such as incessantly rising and falling accompaniment in his *Gretchen am Spinnrade* (Gretchen at the Spinning Wheel).

AND BOB, I'VE GOT THE MUSIC IN ME, TOO.

ROBERT & CLARA SCHUMANN

The first major successor in German lied to Schubert was Robert Schumann (1810-1856), who once wrote more than 120 songs in a single year, his self-proclaimed "Year of Song." Many of his songs were on the subject of love, such as his song cycles *Dichterliebe* (A Poet's Love) and *Frauenliebe und – leben* (Woman's Love and Life), and this inspiration mostly liked stemmed from his upcoming marriage to Clara. Schumann's songs expressed the range of emotions that come with love, and he sought to synthesize two of his greatest interests: music and poetry. As an added bonus, he was able to make a considerable amount of money from what was proving to be a very lucrative genre of music! Like Schubert, Schumann firmly believed that the music should capture the essence of the poem. In contrast to Schubert, he aimed for independence of the accompaniment from the melody; rather, the voice and the piano were equal partners, and he demonstrated this by giving long introductions, interludes, and post-ludes to the piano.

Coming in a close second in popularity to the lied was piano music, which served for piano pedagogy, amateur enjoyment, and pub-lic performance, with many piano works serving more than one of these purposes. Schubert enjoyed success in composing a number of piano works for the amateur market, most of which were short lyrical pieces with a distinctive mood. Schubert also composed a number of piano duets, as well as piano sonatas, although he seemed to struggle with the larger multimovement and expanded musical forms. It would be fair to say that Schubert is much more highly regarded as a composer of vocal music than as a composer of piano music.

Schumann, on the other hand, enjoyed success in composing in both genres. In fact, all of his publications until 1840, "The Year of Song," were for solo piano. Although he composed a few extended piano works, the majority of his compositions were short, character pieces grouped into collections with fanciful titles like *Papillons* (Butterflies) and Car-naval (Carnival). As suggested by the titles, Schumann wanted his listeners to associ-ate his music with extramusical imagery. His piano music reflects contradictions in Schumann's own personality, fervent and dreamy, whimsical and learned.

Two of the most prolific composers of piano music in the Roman-tic period include Fry-deryk Chopin and Franz Liszt, both non-Germans. Chopin (1810-1849) was born near Warsaw to a Polish mother and

FRYDERYK CHOPIN

French father. His early education was in Warsaw and Vienna, and his music reflected both influences, as well as a French style after meeting leading musicians in Paris. In all, his entire output includes about 200 solo piano pieces, in addition to larger works for piano and orchestra, about twenty songs, and a few chamber works. While he wrote study pieces for amateurs, their scope and technical demands made them challenging and appropriate for public performance. Such works were known as concert *études.*

In addition to his famed études, Chopin is also well-known for his dance pieces for solo piano, namely his waltzes, mazurkas, and polonaises. Often composed for his students, these works were incredibly idiomatic to play, and they could make even amateur pianists feel a sense of accomplishment and pride. While his waltzes evoke images of Viennese ballrooms, his mazurkas and polonaises are distinctly Polish in character. Chopin's nocturnes are some of the most beautiful piano works composed, with melodies soaring above rich harmonies in a short mood piece.

While Chopin was known as a composer and outstanding teacher, Franz Liszt (1811-1886) was known as the most prolific piano virtuoso of his time. Like Mozart, Liszt was a child prodigy in Hungary and Vienna, eventually traveling with his family to Paris at the age of twelve. Demand for performances led Liszt to give more than one thousand solo concerts across both Western and Eastern Europe. The first pianist to perform as a soloist in a concert hall, Liszt ultimately created what we know of today as the recital. His music was inspired by both Hungarian and Romanian rhapsodies, and his compositions are among the most technically demanding in the genre.

HEY, I KNEW WHICH END OF THE PIANO TO BANG.

FRANZ LISZT

Chapter 22

THE DEVELOPMENT OF CHAMBER, CHORAL, AND ORCHESTRAL MUSIC

In the nineteenth century, we saw incredible growth of public performances in concert settings. Amateur performances in the public arena abounded under the formation of choral societies and amateur orchestras. At the same time, chamber music—which was once composed and performed exclusively for the private enjoyment of the musicians themselves—now was often performed as concert music. These changes precipitated the standardization of the classical repertoire, beginning first in choral music with the oratorios of Handel and Haydn, followed by the string quartets and symphonies of Haydn,

Mozart, and Beethoven, known collectively as the *First Viennese School.*

Composers of chamber music in the nineteenth century were unable to escape the successful past of their predecessors. Chamber music in concerts was approached with the level of seriousness as the symphonies, especially if they had any connection with the composers of the First Viennese School. Composers more and more commonly sought to match the individuality and creativity of Beethoven's middle and late quartets. Schubert wrote a number of string quartets for the enjoyment of his friends and family, and he often modeled them after those of Mozart and Haydn. He demonstrated his individual and whimsical style in his five-movement quintet for piano, violin, viola, cello, and bass known as the *Trout Quintet.* It received this nickname because of the set of variations on his song *The Trout* in the fourth movement of the work. His *String Quintet in C Major,* composed in the last two months of his life, is revered as one of his greatest achievements in chamber music.

HEY GUYS, YOU'RE SUPPOSED TO BE UP HERE.

Felix Mendelssohn (1809-1847), who composed in a number of popular genres, wrote a considerable amount of chamber music. Mendelssohn was much like Beethoven in that he matured by testing his own skills against those of the masters, and then proved his own mastery by writing in a personal and individual musical language. One of his earliest lauded masterpieces is his *Octet for Strings, Op. 20.* His string quartets between 1827 and 1829 were heavily influenced by the late quartets of Beethoven, achieving continuity throughout the movements while each maintained its own distinct flavor.

Robert Schumann followed his years writing lieder with a "chamber music year" from 1842-1843. Like many others, Schumann studied the string quartets of Mozart and Haydn and fashioned his own with theirs as models while building on their tradition. By the middle of the 1800s, chamber music was viewed as an extension of the more conservative classical style, and while embraced by many, it was rejected by more radical composers like Berlioz and Liszt. Despite the associations with classical style and form, Romantic compositions in chamber most definitely projected their own new and distinctive style and interpretation.

In contrast to the increasingly professional make-up of orchestras, choirs in the nineteenth century were becoming increasingly the domain of amateur musicians. This increase was noticeable both in the church, as well as in choruses outside of the church that were organized by the singers themselves for their own enjoyment. The local amateur choruses were known as choral societies, with dues-paying members that supported the purchase of music, payment of a conductor, and other such expenses. These organizations began popping up across in large European and North American cities such as Leipzig, Zurich, Liverpool, and Boston. While choruses were open to members of both genders, all-male choruses were especially popular in France, Germany, and other cities with large populations of Germans.

WE DON'T SING FOR OUR SUPPER— WE SING FOR THE LOVE OF IT.

The oratorios of Handel and Haydn formed the core of the repertoire of the choral societies, with the Handel and Haydn Society formed in 1815 in Boston remaining the oldest active music organization in the United States today. In addition to oratorio, these societies also performed the music of J.S. Bach: the *St. Matthew Passion, St. John Passion,* and *Mass in B Minor.* Soon Felix Mendelssohn was composing his own oratorios, which, like those of Haydn, were modeled after the oratorios of Handel. His most successful oratorios were *St. Paul* and *Elijah.* The availability of large performing forces inspired other composers of the Romantic period to compose works for ensembles of unprecedented size. Hector Berlioz (1803-1869) in composing his *Grande Messe des Morts* (Requiem) called for four hundred singers and instrumentalists, including twenty woodwinds, twelve horns, more than a hundred strings, and four brass ensembles positioned at four corners of the concert stage in the first performance.

MUSIC MUST BE **BiG!** EVEN WHEN YOU ARE SMALL

HECTOR BERLIOZ

For many choral societies, however, such large-scale works were either too large or too expensive to perform. Thus, the *partsong* became the staple of many smaller amateur choirs. These partsongs were similar to the lied in that they were intended primarily for private entertainment, and they explored virtually every subject available at the time, from patriotism to nature. The church also was important vehicle for the promulgation of choral music. It was in the nineteenth century that the term *a cappella* (Italian for "in the chapel") came to mean "unaccompanied," due to the misconception that all music in the papal chapel where Palestrina worked was performed without instrumental accompaniment. Both the Catholic and Protestant churches promoted the composition of new a cappella choral works.

Like choral music, orchestral music was a key component of life in the nineteenth century. Orchestras grew both in number and in size over the course of the century, and they were staffed by both amateur and professional musicians alike. Eventually, playing in an orchestra became a full-time profession for musicians, just as it is today. By the end of the century, most major European and American cities were home to professional orchestras that offered a regular season of concerts, though not all orchestras were full-time. The growth of orchestras in size from about forty players to nearly one hundred also contributed to the growth of the profession and the art.

The orchestra, from its leadership to its concerts to its audience, also changed immensely in the nineteenth century. In the 1700s, orchestras were led by either the harpsichord player or the leader of the violins (today we call this person the concertmaster), but in the nineteenth century orchestras were led by a *conductor* who used a baton to beat time and cue entrances (the use of a baton instead of a large staff also resulted in fewer conducting-related deaths). While the conductor began as simply a leader of the ensembles, eventually the role became an artistic role in its own right. By the middle of the century, conductors gained fame and acclaim for their interpretations of music, and they were considered as virtuosic as the greatest of instrumentalists.

WITH THIS BATON I COMMAND ARMIES, SEND PEOPLE TO HELL, AND OCCASIONALLY TO HEAVEN — HEY, IT'S ALL IN A DAY'S WORK.

While eighteenth-century orchestras catered primarily to city-dwellers and noble families, the nineteenth-century orchestra drew audiences primarily from the middle class, those same people to whom composers would market published music for in-home enjoyment. In fact, because hearing a live orchestral performance was still a fairly rare event, many symphonies, particularly those of Beethoven, were published as arrangements that could be played at home on the piano. Orchestra concerts were exceedingly diverse, often consisting of a symphony, a choral work, a chamber or solo work, and a concluding symphony. The orchestra concert also contributed to the solidification of a permanent classical repertoire that included primarily the works of Mozart, Haydn, and Beethoven. No orchestra concert in the nineteenth century would be complete without a performance of music from the First Viennese School.

Composers like Schubert, Berlioz, and Mendelssohn pioneered a new Romantic idiom in response to the classical repertoire. Schubert, for instance, focused more intently on more tuneful melodies, heightened emotions, and adventurous experiments with harmony and instrumental colors. Berlioz, on the other hand, assumed a different approach by composing programmatic music as his response to the symphony. One of the most inspiring and popular works in music history is his *Symphonie fantastique,* which tells the story of a young man's obsession and infatuation with a woman, whose love he seeks to win. Throughout the composition, Berlioz presents an *idée fixe* (fixed idea), a melody that represents the hero's obsessive love that recurs in various transformations in each movement. The other major contributor to the orchestral symphonic repertoire was Mendelssohn, although his music sounded much more Classical than that of either Berlioz or Schubert.

The first half of the nineteenth century saw, paradoxically, the permanent fixture of the First Viennese School in the classical repertory and the Romantic development of existing genres by the period's leading composers. Music-making was becoming an activity, profession, and entertainment of the middle class, and less an art form restricted only to the noble and wealthy.

Chapter 23

THE FAT
LADY SINGS:
INNOVATION IN ITALIAN
AND GERMAN OPERA

Up until now, the role of opera in the history of music has been largely neglected in this book, not due to its lack of importance, but because of the opposite: its long, lasting, and rich tradition. While most opera history is beyond the scope of this book, opera played such an important role in the music of the nineteenth century that it would be a major oversight to exclude a discussion of the effect it had on not only the opera world, but also music in general. In this chapter we will take a look at the leading composers of opera throughout the century, noting specifically the innovations and developments they contributed to music.

GIAOCHINO ROSSINI

In the first half of the nineteenth century, the leading Italian composers were Rossini, Donizetti, and Bellini, creating new works that have been performed annually since their first performances. Gioachino Rossini (1792-1868) enjoyed immense popularity, fame, and importance throughout Europe, even more so than Beethoven, which is difficult to believe! While he is best known today for his comic operas such as *L'Italiana in Algeri* (The Italian Woman in Algiers) and *Il Barbiere di Siviglia* (The Barber of Seville), his reputation came from serious operas, such as *Otello*. He also is well known for the development of the **bel canto** ("beautiful singing") style, which refers to elegant, fluid, and lyrical delivery of all melodies, with the voice taking precedent over all other elements of the opera, including the orchestra, story, and visuals.

Vincenzo Bellini (1801-1835), a younger contemporary of Rossini, grew in reputation after Rossini's retirement from opera composition. Bellini, who died at the age of thirty-four, composed ten operas in all, of which the best known are *La Sonnambula* (The Sleepwalker), *Norma,* and *I Puritani* (The Puritans). His music is marked by the long-breathed, intensely emotional, and highly ornamental character of his melodies. Gaetano Donizetti (1797-1848) was a contemporary of both Bellini and Rossini, and he proved to be one of the most prolific Italian composers of the early nineteenth century, having composed oratorios, cantatas, chamber and church music, about one hundred songs, and a few symphonies—all of this in addition to his more than seventy operas.

Later in the century, Giuseppe Verdi (1813-1901) would prove to be the dominant composer of Italian music for the fifty years after Donizetti. In all, he composed more than twenty-six operas, including *Rigoletto, La Traviata* (The Fallen Woman), and Falstaff. His music has been described as the epitome of Romanticism, both in drama and passion. While he continued working within established opera traditions, he worked his entire life to put his own mark on the music world. Verdi's heightened sense of drama and passion is seen not only in his operas but in his other works as well. His *Messa da Requiem,* a large-scale choral-orchestral mass for the dead, incorporates many dramatic elements of opera and elevates that genre to a new echelon.

The most important and successful Italian composer of opera after Verdi was Giacomo Puccini (1858-1924). His highly individual personal style blended Verdi's attention to melody and drama with Richard Wagner's approach to recurring melodies (don't worry—we'll discuss Wagner very soon). His operas juxtaposed contrasting musical styles and harmonies to accentuate the contrasting characters in the stories. One of Puccini's most beloved and recognized operas is *La bohème*, a look at the lives of starving artists in the Parisian Latin Quarter. In addition to becoming a staple in opera houses around the world, *La bohème* would go on to influence the hit Broadway musical *Rent*.

Meanwhile in Germany, music and literature were busy interacting, a typical feature of nineteenth-century Romanticism. This ideal was most fully developed in the German-speaking lands in the genres of song, instrumental music, and opera. The opera that established Germany as a contender in the world of Romantic opera was *Der Freischütz* (The Rifleman) by Carl Maria von Weber (1786-1826). The innovative feature of this opera was not only the composer's usual choice of instruments in the orchestra, but also the concept of a story focused on the daily lives of ordinary people. Further emphasizing the Romantic nature of the opera, the libretto dealt with typical Romantic topics of the supernatural and the wilderness as a place of mystery.

Following von Weber was Richard Wagner (1813-1883), one of the most crucial (and infamous) composers in nineteenth-century culture and all of music history. An outstanding composer of German opera, his philosophies transcended music into all areas of the arts, with the arts scene as a sort of religion in and of itself. In music he took German to a new level, he created a new genre called the music drama, and he developed harmonies that eventually influenced composers to abandon tonality entirely.

124

The *music drama* was based on Wagner's philosophy that drama and music were inextricably connected, and the two together organically express a unified dramatic idea. His earlier operas, such as *The Flying Dutchman,* were modeled in the vein of von Weber's operas, but Wagner's famed *Ring Cycle* established the innovative genre he called music drama. Wagner wrote four librettos for a cycle of four operas with the collective title of *Der Ring des Nibelungen* (The Ring of the Nibelungs). His operas had a sense of continuity not only because of the music-drama union, but also because of his use of the **Leitmotiv,** a recurring theme or musical motive that is associated with a character or subject. One of the best examples of the power of the leitmotive is Wagner's opera *Tristan und Isolde,* which tells the story of a secret love incited by a potion that ultimately leads to the lovers' demise.

Although now widely performed in opera houses, public and critical reception of *Tristan und Isolde* was initially quite unfavorable. Why? Wagner in many ways abandoned many aspects of tonality, the system of harmonies that had defined Western art music for the past two hundred and fifty years. Reactions ranged from utter disgust (Clara Schumann wrote that the opera was "the most repugnant thing I have ever seen or heard in all my life.") to negative visceral reaction (German Bohemian music critic Eduard Hanslick said that it "reminds one of the old Italian painting of a martyr whose intestines are slowly unwound from his body on a reel." Wagner's contrasts between tonally stable and unstable passages of music were the hallmark of his compositional language, and his ideals would have a more far-reaching effect than he might have imagined.

Chapter 24

BRAHMS AND THE WAGNERIANS

usic composed after the middle of the nineteenth century might seem to be more diverse than that of earlier eras due to the more careful preservation of historical data; however, that diversity was indeed the case, and only the twentieth century would eclipse the late 1800s in diversity of musical styles, forms, and genres. Before the nineteenth century, the music performed was by living composers, or at most a composer who had died within a few decades; rarely did the performance of a composer's music survive beyond a generation. By the middle of the nineteenth century, choral, chamber, and orchestra concerts consisted increasingly of the established classical repertoire.

The older music of the First Viennese School was here to stay, and this posed a major conundrum for composers in the mid-1800s: what path should they follow? Should they continue composing in the established idioms of Mozart, Haydn, and Beethoven, while adding their own innovations and flare to the recognizable precedents as Johannes Brahms did? Or should they guide their music in a different direction, creating new genres and styles as Wagner and Liszt did? The late nineteenth century was filled with polarizing dichotomies such as absolute versus program music, convention versus novelty, and classical forms and genres versus new ones. Regardless of the direction, it is evident that both sides of the dispute sought to link their works with the legacy of Beethoven.

When Johannes Brahms (1833-1897) was a mere twenty years old, sixty percent of all concert music was that of dead composers; by age forty that number was closer to eighty percent. Brahms elected to follow the path of the masters and sought to compose works that would rival their compositions while providing something fresh and innovative. He not only admired the work of composers like Bach and Beethoven, but also found inspiration in their music for his own creations. Brahms spent nearly twenty years composing his first symphony, knowing well he was standing in the shadow of the great Beethoven. Brahms once stated, "You have no idea how someone like me feels when he hears such a giant marching behind him all the time." Indeed, Beethoven was a giant, but so was Brahms. In fact, he is commonly considered to be Beethoven's successor. His first symphony in C minor was in many ways modeled after Beethoven, but produced music that was distinctly Romantic. The final movement, which concludes in C major like Beethoven's *Fifth Symphony*, is a clear homage to Beethoven—Brahms interpolates and reworks the "Ode to Joy" melody of Beethoven's *Ninth Symphony*.

Brahms was Beethoven's true successor not only in orchestral music, but also in chamber music. His output of twenty-four chamber works is not nearly as impressive as the painstaking quality that each exhibits. In his chamber works and symphonies alike, one can distinctly hear the influence of earlier models in a language that is clearly identifiable as Brahms'. Brahms wrote a number of extraordinary works in the genres of piano music (developing his own imaginative style), song (using the Lieder of Schubert as a model), and choral music (inspired by the music of Heinrich Schütz and Bach). One of the greatest all-time compositions is Brahms' *Ein Deutsches Requiem* (A German Requiem), composed for soprano and baritone soloists, chorus, and orchestra. The influence of Bach and Schütz is evident in Brahms' imitative treatment of vocal parts and in the text expressivity. While inspired by older models, the work is groundbreaking in the text chosen: instead of using the Latin Mass for the Dead, Brahms compiled texts drawn from the Old Testament, Apocrypha, and New Testament. It is well known that Brahms composed this not as a mass for the dead, but as a comfort for the living.

JOHANNES
BRAHMS

While it may seem that Brahms' music was conservative at the time, he actually was a trailblazer, setting traditional inherited forms in his own idiom and language. At the same time, another branch of composers who sought to break from the past was emerging. Music critic Franz Brendel grouped leading music innovators Liszt, Wagner, and Berlioz together in what he called the *"New German School."* This might not make much sense, given that neither Berlioz nor Liszt were German, but Brendel was referring to the fact that all sought to follow in the footsteps of Beethoven, which makes their music German in origin. These and other composers were considered Wagnerian in that they followed Wagner's new path away from the classical repertoire.

HE AIN'T HEAVY,
HE'S MY WAGNER.
WELL, AT LEAST
MY SON-IN-LAW.

Surprisingly, one of the earliest Wagnerian's was Franz Liszt, who, after retiring from his career as a touring pianist, focused his efforts on composition while working as the court music director at Weimar. Because he was no longer composing works simply to demonstrate his virtuosic talent, Liszt was able to free himself of the established tradition. He created a new genre of orchestral music that he called the *symphonic poem,* a one-movement programmatic work that was suggested by a picture, play, poem, or other art form. Analogous to the literary poem, Liszt's new genre fell in line with Wagner's philosophy of a collective artwork.

Viennese composer Anton Bruckner (1824-1896) not only shared Wagner's outlook on music, but also sought to fully absorb Wagner's style and musical language in his own orchestral compositions. Like other Wagnerian composers, Bruckner modeled his symphonies on the music of Beethoven, particular the Ninth Symphony, in an effort to achieve the same level of purpose, grandeur, and religious spirit. Bruckner's symphonies also followed Beethoven's lead in the recycling of previously presented musical materials in the final movement. The music of Hugo Wolf (1860-1903), on the other hand, exemplifies the adaption of Wagner's approach to German lied. While Wolf composed music in a number of genres, his greatest success laid in his songs. Producing some two hundred fifty lieder in a period of ten years, Wolf concentrated his efforts on one poet at a time, and he also embraced Wagner's new ideal of equality between words and music. He prescribed to Wagner's philosophy of a collective artwork, successfully fused music and poetry, and achieved a balance between piano and voice that required neither to be subordinate to the other.

While each of the composers in this chapter followed a different path, all were successful in the path they chose to follow. Brahms composed music in a wide variety of traditional forms and genres, paying homage to Bach, Handel, and the First Viennese School. Other composers who prescribed to Wagnerian wing of music, focused more narrowly on specific genres while following Wagner's lead in the collective artwork, form, and harmony.

BUCKING THE TREND: MUSIC IN THE 20TH CENTURY

Chapter 25

IS IT LATE ROMANTIC OR MODERN?

The early twentieth century saw numerous changes in the areas of technology, society, and the arts, music in particular. Seeking to secure their spot in the permanent classical repertoire and fighting for space on concert programs with the "old" music, composers felt the need to offer a unique style and voice that struck a balance between conventional and new elements. Each composer came up with a unique solution to this dilemma, differing greatly in what each kept and rejected from past traditions and the innovations they created.

By 1900, the classical repertoire of Mozart, Haydn, and Beethoven had secured their place in history and in the concert hall, with everything from orchestral music to chamber music, to solo repertoire for piano or voice being performed. The expectations of players and audience members alike had drastically changed since the eighteenth century, when they always desired something new and innovative and anything more than a few decades old was considered unfashionable. By the twentieth century, audiences were demanding music that was at least a generation old, and new music was judged against the masterworks of the permanent classical repertoire. This is the challenge that composers in the first half of the twentieth century faced: how to compete against the classics for the attention of performers and audiences who were enamored with  those traditional masterworks while creating something unique and distinguished that would forever hold a place in the permanent repertoire.

Composers in Germany and Austria (both German-speaking countries) faced perhaps the greatest challenge of all composers, given that the standard-bearers' music was German. Of all German composers of their Generation, Gustav Mahler and Richard Strauss were the most successful, each finding their own way of building upon the inherited traditions while creating a music that was both innovative and familiar. Mahler (1860-1911) was the leading composers of symphonies, following Brahms and Bruckner. Although he started his career as a dynamic, precise, and expressive conductor, he eventually turned to composition, mainly in the summers between conducting seasons. It was during this time that he composed his five orchestral song cycles and nine symphonies, with a tenth symphony left unfinished.

As a composer of symphonies, Mahler drew upon the foundation created by Beethoven, using the symphony as a vehicle for a bold, highly personal statement. Mahler once said that the job of the composer in a symphony was "to construct a world," and his symphonies often feel filled with life experience, telling a story or recreating a visual scene. Mahler also created his own unique style through his choice of instruments. Typically his works demand an incredibly large cadre of performers. For example, his *Second Symphony* calls for an enormous section of strings, seventeen woodwinds, twenty-five brass instruments, six timpani plus additional percussion, four harps, organ, soprano and alto soloists, and a large chorus. His *Eighth Symphony* demanded even larger forces, earning itself the nickname "Symphony of a Thousand."

GUSTAV
MAHLER

While Mahler's symphonies usually were programmatic and revolved around some type of program, his orchestral song cycles were truly a collective artwork that would inspired Wagner. His haunting *Kindertotenlieder* (Songs on the Death of Children) is set to the poetry of Friedrich Rückert. In the *Kindertotenlieder,* Mahler continues in Wagner's musical language of creating stark contrast between consonant and dissonant sounds and unstable, shifting tonalities, creating an ironic, understated restraint given that the subject is the death of one's child. In his *Das Lied von der Erde* (The Song of the Earth), Mahler drew not upon German poetry but upon translations of Chinese poetry. In this work, Mahler achieves a perfect balance between the orchestra and singers, a Wagnerian ideal.

While Mahler chose to follow Beethoven by composing song cycles and symphonies, Richard Strauss (1864-1949) followed a different path: having established himself as the successful heir of composing symphonic poems after Liszt, Strauss shifted his compositional efforts to opera in an effort to inherit Wagner's new style. While his first two operas were mediocre at best, Strauss hit a home run with his *Salome* in 1905. A one-act play by Oscar Wilde in German translation, the opera tells the biblical story of Salome, who performs her famous Dance of the Seven Veils to persuade Herod to deliver the head of John the Baptist on a silver platter so that she might kiss his cold, dead lips. This was by far the most bizarre opera ever in subject matter, and Strauss used this to his advantage by composing in a complex and dissonant style. In this opera and in his immensely popular *Der Rosenkavalier* (The Cavalier of the Rose), Strauss aimed to appeal directly to the emotions of the audience.

RICHARD STRAUSS

I FEEL GOOD!

CLAUDE DEBUSSY

A well-known composer these days, Claude Debussy (1862-1918) chose not to extend the Wagnerian tradition as Mahler and Strauss did; rather, he delighted in the moment. His work is often associated with impressionism (analogous to the impressionist painters), but his music is actually closer to symbolism. French impressionism in art was characterized by the works of painters such as Claude Monet, in which artists sought not to portray things as they were in reality, but as the impressions given to the artist. Symbolism, a contemporary artistic movement, was reflected in the poetry of such greats as Paul Verlaine and Stéphane Mallarmé, whose poetry used intense imagery, disrupted syntax, and symbols to effect a dreamlike state to suggest emotions and experiences rather than stating them directly. Debussy knew these poets' work well, and he often used their texts for his songs and dramatic works.

Debussy's music is all about atmosphere, evoking a mood, feeling, or scene through individual images that carry the work's meaning and structure. One can hear this clearly in Debussy's famous *Claire de lune* ("Moonlight"), which is based on a poem of the same name by Paul Verlaine. His style is also evident in his orchestral piece *Prélude à "L'après-midi d'un faune"* (Prelude to "The Afternoon of a Faun"), which he based on symbolist poem by Mallarmé, and in which he evokes mood through suggestion and indirections instead of direct emotional appeal or expression. While Debussy's music stretches tonality to new limits at times, his status as a late Romantic or early Modern composer is ambiguous and unclear.

The beginning of the twentieth also produced a number of composers who were clearly members of the first generation of modern music. Their music clearly absorbed the traditions of the past, but their personal style and language were so unique, distinctive, and individual that they can hardly be called late Romanticists. One such composer was Maurice Ravel (1875-1937), a French composer who is often associated with the impressionism of Debussy, but whose music is far more modern. In many ways, he was a master assimilator, absorbing and reworking a variety of influences in all his music. In England, Ralph Vaughan Williams (1872-1958) and Gustav Holst (1874-1934) established a new English musical renaissance. Vaughan Williams incorporated English folk music in many of his works, while Holst looked also to other sources, such as Hindu sacred texts in his *Choral Hymns from the Rig Veda.* Nationalism and innovation also inspired the music of Czech composer Leoš Janáček, Finnish composer Jean Sibelius, Spain's Manuel de Falla, and Russia's Sergi Rachmaninov.

MAURICE RAVEL

Opinions have changed many times about the composers of classical repertoire in the early twentieth century. Like the music of past eras that blurred the boundaries between those periods, the music of the early twentieth century served as a bridge between the monumental figures of the late Romantic period and the truly modern composers that we will learn about in the next chapter. All of the composers in this time display characteristics of both late Romanticism and early Modernism, which is perhaps why the music of Mahler, Sibelius, Ravel, Debussy, Rachmaninov, and Strauss have cemented their place in the classical repertoire with extremely popular music.

Chapter 26

THROWING THE BABY OUT WITH THE BATHWATER: SCHOENBERG AND FRIENDS

*A*round the time of World War I, a group of young composers would leave an indelible print on the music world, forging a radical new path that broke away from the musical language of their predecessors (and contemporaries). At the same time, they managed to maintain some strong ties to tradition. Like modernists in art who pioneered expressionism, cubism, and abstract art, these composers prescribed to *modernism*, too; their goal was not to please or entice listeners upon first hearing one of their works. Instead, they aimed to challenge the status quo and provide an experience that could not be

achieved through the traditional
idiom. The modernist composers unhesi-
tatingly claimed the great composers of the past as their
model, even though this seems contradictory. They viewed themselves
as continuing the innovative work of the iconic classical composers, not
radically overthrowing tradition. To many listeners, however, this is
exactly what these modernist composers did.

The leader, teacher, and founder of the modernist movement was
German composer Arnold Schoenberg (1874-1951). While he initially
composed works in a late Romantic style, he eventually moved beyond
the establish tonal system to *atonality*—a term in music that describes
the avoidance of a tonal center (i.e. establishing one pitch as the most
important or "home" pitch of a work). Although Schoenberg did not
particularly care for the term atonal, it is a proper word to describe his
abandonment of tonality. Because music had grown increasingly dissonant in the past fifty years, Schoenberg felt that a tonal center was an
arbitrary designation and therefore useless. His music allowed for what

he called "the emancipation of the dissonance"—where dissonance is free to exist in its own right without the necessity of resolving to a consonant sonority.

While his first atonal works were freely atonal (that is, no set method to determining the pitches), Schoenberg eventually developed a composition called the *twelve-tone row*. *Serial music,* as it was also called, was based on assigning a number to each of twelve pitches and then creating a matrix that demonstrated a number of combinatorial possibilities without repeating a number. Using the matrix, a composer would use the rows from that matrix as a method for composing a work. Another popular innovation by Schoenberg was *Sprechstimme* ("speaking voice") in which a singer did not accurately sing the pitches on the page; rather, he or she would approximate those written pitches in a speech-like tone while following the rhythm exactly. His cycle of twenty-one songs called *Pierrot lunaire* (Moonstruck Pierrot), which was drawn from a larger poetic cycle by Belgian symbolist poet Albert Giraud, best exemplifies both atonality and sprechstimme in a single work.

Despite his relatively small space in music history, Arnold Schoenberg deserves a notable place in history and this book because of his thinking, compositions, and approaches to music influenced music for the rest of the twentieth century. Additionally, he created an unprecedentedly complex musical language and influenced other composers enormously, especially his students Alban Berg and Anton Webern. Together the three of them were referred to as the *Second Viennese School.* Berg (1885-1935) began his musical studies with Schoenberg at the age of nineteen. Although he gladly subscribed to Schoenberg's atonal and twelve-tone methods, listeners often found Berg's music much more idiomatic and understandable (and occasionally pleasant!). His opera *Wozzeck* is one such example; the music is atonal and includes some use of sprechstimme while employing leitmotives and traditional forms.

GOES WITH PEAS.

ALBAN BERG

His colleague Anton Webern (1883-1945) began studying with Schoenberg in 1904, the same year that Berg began his studies with the radical composer. Webern deeply held a music philosophy that music had the capability of expressing ideas that no other medium was capable of. Furthermore, he believed that great art develops out of necessity, not arbitrarily; that evolution in art was a must; and that musical practices and styles can only progress, not regress. He viewed each step in music history as an act of discovery, not invention, and these deeply held beliefs gave him—and his teacher—great confidence in their music. Like Schoenberg and Berg, Webern passed through stages of late Romanticism, atonality, and eventually serial music.

On the other end of the modernist spectrum were composers who sought to compose innovative music with the flavor of their own national tradition and heritage. Aside from Igor Stravinsky (about whom we will learn in the next chapter), two of the most significant were the Hungarian Béla Bartók and American Charles Ives. Bartók (1881-1945) was a piano teacher, pianist, ethnomusicologist, and leading composer of the early twentieth century. In his compositions, he synthesized the peasant and folk music of Eastern Europe (namely Hungary, Romania, Slovakia, and Bulgaria) with the elements inherent in classical German and French music. Bartók spent his lifetime traveling Eastern Europe in search of folk songs and dances, which he collected thousands of. He used his collection to arrange folk tunes and to compose pieces based on them.

Charles Ives (1874-1954) was like Bartók in that his own modernist style is characterized by synthesis; in Ives' case, it was the synthesis of both international and regional traditions in music. Ives based his compositions on four distinct styles of music with which he was intimately familiar: American folk music, Protestant church music, Western European classical music, and experimental music. As a child, Ives grew up surrounded by not only the popular music of the time (such as marches, parlor songs, and show tunes), but also Protestant hymns heard in church at revival meetings. For most of his teens and twenties Ives was a professional church organist (he later went on to become an insurance salesman). As an organist, Ives was surrounded by the great composers of organ music like Bach and Mendelssohn, and his musical studies at Yale led him to study the music of many other masters. In his *experimental music,* Ives approached the traditional rules of music by keeping most of them while changing others to see what would happen. As a child he practiced drumming on the piano, playing particular pitches to see if he could imitate the sound of drums. In his symphonies, sonatas, and other works, Ives combined all of these musical styles into a musical collage, all of them intricately woven together to create an idiom unique to Ives.

CHARLES IVES

IGOR STRAVINSKY

(YES, HE DESERVES

HIS OWN CHAPTER)

*I*gor Stravinsky (1882-1971) was an important part of the most significant musical trends in musical modernism. He composed some of the most successful and lasting compositions of the twentieth century, and he greatly influenced the next three generations of composers. In fact, some scholars have asserted that all music composed in the twentieth century after Stravinsky can, in some way, be traced back to Stravinsky as an influential model. Not only did Stravinsky compose a host of works that have become a part of the classical music canon, but also he composed a variety of music styles and idioms, each of which he displayed complete mastery.

Stravinsky's first compositional style is known as his Russian period.

Born near St. Petersburg in Russia, it is no wonder that his first attempts at composition were rooted in the national styles of his motherland. His most popular early works were all ballets *(The Firebird, Petrushka,* and *The Rite of Spring),* works composed for Sergei Diaghilev, head of the Ballets Russes in Paris. *The Firebird* was based on Russian folk tales, and the composition follows a style common of his teacher, Nikolai Rimsky-Korsakov. *Petrushka* began to show hints of a Stravinskian Russian style, but *The Rite of Spring* was the ballet that truly set Stravinsky apart from his contemporaries. The subject of the ballet was Russian, but it was set in prehistoric Russia and imagined an ancient ritual in which an adolescent girl would be selected to sacrifice herself by dancing herself to death. The entire composition is marked by a style called primitivism, a style that was crude, uncultured, and base. The premiere of *The Rite of Spring* is notorious for the riot that broke out in the audience, who were shocked by this new style called *primitivism.* Spectators hissed and booed at the music's "primitive" evocation of pagan fertility rites, its harshly insistent dissonance, its percussiveness, and its pounding rhythms. Eventually the piece would become one of the most frequently performed modern compositions.

OH YEAH, SPRING IS ALWAYS EVERYONES' FAVORITE 'TIL IT'S TIME TO SACRIFICE SOMEBODY.

IGOR STRAVINSKY

Stravinsky's second period, later to be called his Neoclassical Period, came about when Diaghilev asked Stravinsky to orchestrate a number of pieces by eighteenth-century composer Pergolesi for a new ballet called *Pulcinella.* Instead of simply taking the source material and setting it for orchestra, Stravinsky applied his own distinct musical language while retaining the essence of the original music. Stravinsky called this experience a "discovery of the past," and it led him to compose a number of other works in a neoclassical style. *Neoclassicism* has come to be understood as a broad movement in the first third of the nineteenth century in which composers revived, emulated, or recalled forms, genres, and stylistic traits of music before the Romantic period. Stravinsky was considered the leader of this neoclassical movement that rejected Romanticism and yearned for the past in the wake of World War I.

Stravinsky composed a number of pieces in this neoclassical style, including his Mass for choir and double wind quintet, his only opera (*The Rake's Progress),* a number of oratorios including *Oedipus Rex,* and the famous *Symphony of Psalms.* A masterpiece from Stravinsky's neoclassical period, *Symphony of Psalms* was commissioned by the Boston Symphony Orchestra in celebration of its 50th anniversary. It has three movements and is scored for chorus and orchestra. Stravinsky wanting to create the sound of an "organ that breathes," and thus employed a very large and unorthodox combination of orchestral instruments: Four flutes, one piccolo, four oboes, one English horn, three bassoons, one contrabassoon, four horns, five trumpets, three trombones, one tuba, timpani, bass drum, harp, two pianos, cellos, double basses, and choir (note that there are no treble string instruments, e.g. violin and viola).

I MAY BE RUSSIAN BUT I DO LOVE A GOOD SMORGASBORD.

Following Wagner's lead, Stravinsky wanted the voices and instruments to be on equal terms, with neither one outweighing the other.

The three movements are related by musical motives and are performed without interruption. Stravinsky used the term symphony not in its usual sense, but simply to indicate a work in several movements that calls for an orchestra, with each movement based on a psalm from the Latin Vulgate Bible: Psalms 38, 39, and 150. Because of the religious nature of this work, Stravinsky devoted each movement to one of St. Paul's hortatory virtues: love, hope, and faith. Stravinsky chose the Latin version of the psalms to evoke the feeling of an ancient and solemn ritual. An austere, archaic quality is also communicated through the chant-like melodies that are sometimes restricted to only one or two pitches. Furthermore, Stravinsky captured the Baroque ideal of perpetual motion, in which there seems to be no rest for the music.

After Schoenberg's death in 1951, Stravinsky finally embraced the atonal and twelve-tone methods that had become a large part of the modernist musical language. Stravinsky waited until after Schoenberg's death to begin composing serial music because he feared he could never live up to the standard Schoenberg had set. One his best known serial works is his song cycle *In memoriam Dylan Thomas*. Stravinsky's genius was evident in his ability to take any musical style or idiom and add his own distinctive traits to it. His music became an example for other composers of modern music, and the scope of his influence remains to be seen.

MUSIC AND
POSTMODERNISM

$\mathcal{I}$n the years following World War II, the tradition of classical music performance grew stronger than ever. Concert attendance, government support, expansion of schools of music, and music education in primary and secondary schools all saw dramatic growth. In contrast, the living composers who considered themselves heirs of the classical music tradition found themselves further and further disconnected from society, as if they were composing in a vacuum. They also found little common ground amongst themselves in regard to approach, style, aesthetic, or purpose in their music. Some of them focused on retaining some semblance of perceived tradition in order to appeal to audiences, while others created completely new traditions.

While a few composers, like Stravinsky, were able to make a living from composing new works, conducting, or giving other performances, for the majority of composers this was not the case. In Europe the patronage of music by the aristocracy and of royalty had come to an end, and thus composers had to seek new forms of patronage. Support for composers in Europe came via the state, radio stations, annual subsidies, grants, and educational institutions. In the United States, composers found support for their work as well as steady employment in higher education, with many composers accepting faculty positions at universities, colleges, and conservatories. In particular, centers of music and scholarship were established on the west coast at the University of California and Mills College, on the east coast at Yale University, and in the Midwest at the Universities of Illinois, Indiana, and Michigan.

While there was an immense of amount of music composed between the world wars and afterwards, this chapter will focus on a survey of the composers who contributed to a postmodernist style. Postmodernism was a reactive movement in the arts, architecture, and literature that grew out of Modernism and most accurately describes an opposition to it. Composers like Milton Babbit (1916-2011) and Pierre Boulez

I AM NOT A SERIAL KILLER, BUT MY SERIAL MUSIC KILLS, TOTALLY!

MILTON BABBITT

(b. 1925) were part of a movement that grew out of modernism, particularly in regards to serialism. Babbit, for instance, applied the musical methods of serialism to all aspects of music (not just pitch) in what has been termed total serialism. *Total serialism* assumes that if pitches can be systematically applied, then so could other musical elements such as duration, intensity, volume, and timbre. French composer Pierre Boulez created the first European work of total serialism, *Structures*, in which duration and pitch are serialized, while dynamics and articulations delineated the musical form. While totally serial musical compositions may sound unpredictable and random to the listener, they actually are highly systematized and structured works of music.

On the other end of the serial spectrum were composers like Luciano Berio (1925-2003) and Elliott Carter (1908-2012), who explored complex and virtuosic musical styles without serialism. Completely serial compositions were exceedingly difficult to perform, as even the difference in volume between loud and very loud determined correct or incorrect performance of a work. Both Berio and Carter used non-serial, atonal language, and their works were complex because they required a highly developed performance technique and musical prowess.

In a break from the methodological approach to innovation in music, other composers focused on developing new instruments and sounds through the discovery of world instruments, the modification of existing traditional Western instruments, and even the invention of entirely new instruments! One such composer who focused on a new approach to instruments and sounds was American composer John Cage (1912-1992). Cage wrote a number of works for percussion ensembles for both traditional instruments and untraditional ones, like tin cans and electric buzzers. His work in sound exploration culminated with the *prepared piano:* a piano would be prepared with various items—such as bolts, pennies, wood, plastic, or rubber—placed between the strings, resulting in a unique timbre when played from the keyboard. George Crumb (b. 1929) is highly regarded for his ability to extract new sounds out of common instruments and objects. For example, his works would include unorthodox sources like toy piano, Tibetan singing bowls, harmonica, and musical saw. Like Cage, he also applied prepared techniques to the piano, harp, and mandolin while exploring extended techniques on string instruments. Other composers looked to synthesized sounds, recorded sounds, and other electronically-created sounds as the canvas for their art.

In the late twentieth-century, music began to be seen as spatial, with masses of sound moving through space and interacting with each other. This idea of music as a spatial texture was pioneered with acoustic instruments first by Greek composer Iannis Xenakis (1922-2001). He spent most of his career in France not only as a composer, but also as an engineer and architect, vocations that likely influenced his thoughts on music and space. His day jobs also influenced his philosophy that mathematics was the foundation of music, and thus based much of his music on mathematical concepts and procedures. Polish composer Krzysztof Penderecki (b. 1933) also prescribed to the school of texture and process. His work is best exemplified in his *Threnody to the Victims of Hiroshima*

THIS IS MUSIC TO EVOLVE BY.

for fifty-two string instruments, in which musical time is measured not with pulses but in seconds and in which each individual instrument has a unique part to play. György Ligeti (1923-2006) gained his fame through Stanley Kubrick's science fiction film *2001: A Space Odyssey.* The film features excerpts of several of Ligeti's compositions, all of which are characterized by both constant motion and, paradoxically, stasis.

One more important postmodernist movement in musical composition was led by John Cage, who avant-garde philosophies included experiencing sounds not as a vehicle for a composer's expression but for the sake of the sounds themselves. His main strategies for achieving this avant-garde approach were chance, indeterminacy, and obscuring the boundaries of music, art, and life. *Chance* is exactly what it sounds like: the music leaves some aspects of performances to chance; that is, decisions that normally would be made by the composers were left up to the performers in the moment of performance. *Indeterminacy* is similar in that the composer simply leaves certain aspects of the music unspecified. Cage's most extreme work of indeterminacy was his most famous piece: *4'33"* (Four Minutes Thirty-Three Seconds). In the work, a performer would enter the concert hall and remain on stage without producing a single sound; the performance would consist of whatever ambient noises were produced in the concert hall or from the outside.

It is likely that the reader has not heard of many of the composers or works described in this chapter, as postwar classical music has not fared very well, especially in comparison to its popular counterparts of jazz, rock, and musical theatre. While it is reasonable to say that the majority of these works have not entered the classical repertoire of Bach, Beethoven, and Stravinsky, the pioneering of avant-garde composers like John Cage has indeed influenced future composers, such as in the field of film music.

Chapter 29

Y2K:

IT'S NOT AS BAD AS

THEY THOUGHT IT WOULD BE

The end of the millennium brought about a changing world of music, with globalization playing a key role in the expansion and development of other types of music as art music. The term *art music* itself broadened, encompassing not only the work of Bach, Mozart, and Beethoven, but also music from the jazz repertoire, rock and roll, and musical theatre. One indication of this is the role of these types of music in education, with all of them serving as areas of scholarly research and publishing. Globalization has also expanded the appetite of listeners, with many now becoming aware of and interested in East Asian music.

One of the most popular trends in what we will continue to call classical music has been *minimalism,* a compositional technique in which musical materials (i.e. pitches, rhythms, etc.) are kept to a minimum and simplified so that music itself is transparent and obvious. Minimalism can also be seen in the visual arts, as well as in the culinary art of gastronomy, where complex dishes are reduced down to their most basic components. Three American composers have contributed the most to bring minimalism to a broad artist: Steve Reich (b. 1936), Philip Glass (b. 1937) and John Adams (b. 1947). They all have enjoyed success in their own right: Reich with his own music ensembles, Glass primarily in film music, and Adams almost exclusively in the classical vein.

Towards the end of the twentieth century, composers were faced with the reality that in order to obtain performances for their works, they must find a way to make it more accessible for audiences. While it was relatively easy for a composer to receive a commission for the premiere of a new work, securing subsequent performances was a difficult feat. At the same time, audiences for classical music seemed to be dwindling, with long-standing orchestras even shutting their doors due to budgetary shortfalls. Minimalism was one solution to the accessibility dilemma, while for others the answer was *polystylism* (a combination of old and new styles through direct quotation or stylistic allusion), *neo-Romanticism* (an adoption of the expressive toolbox from the Romantic period), and the invocation of extramusical imagery and meanings.

It is too early to say what music of the last seventy-five years will be remembered by music history, which pieces will enter the permanent repertoire of classical music. While there does not appear to be a leading figure in this time period, it just might be good thing for music. With advances in technology encouraging the constant creation and dissemination of new music, it is no longer necessary to focus our listening on just a few great composers.

Glossary

a cappella: the singing of choral music without instrumental accompaniment.

absolute music: music that is independent of any kind of representational aspect, such as words, drama, or visual images.

aria: a term that generally means a song for a solo singer; the term changes in meaning over time.

Ars Nova: term used to describe a new musical style in fourteenth-century France that was marked by innovations in rhythmic notation, melodic patterning, and the standardization of song forms.

atonality: term for music that avoids establishing a pitch or chord as the central sonority.

ballata: a fourteenth-century Italian secular song originally intended to accompany dancing.

basso continuo: a convention developed in the Baroque period, in which composers wrote out a melody and bass line, with performers of the bass line left to fill in the appropriate harmonies.

basso ostinato: also known as ground bass, it is a composition method where a short pattern in the bass would be repeated continuously over an ever-changing melody and harmony above it.

bel canto: a style of singing developed in nineteenth-century opera that is based on the elegant, fluid, and lyrical delivery of all melodies, with the voice taking precedent over all other elements of the opera.

binary form: a form consisting of two parts.

cadenza: an extended elaborately-decorated passage of music demonstrating the virtuosity of a performer.

cantata: a genre of vocal music whose meaning changes over time; in the early seventeenth century, it was a secular form for solo voice accompanied by instruments. In the eighteenth century it refers to a form of Lutheran church music.

cantillation: the chanting of sacred texts.

cantus firmus: an existing melody, often chant, on which a polyphonic composition is based.

cantus-firmus mass: a polyphonic mass in which a melody recurs in a single voice.

chacona: a seventeenth-century lively dance-song form brought from Latin America to Spain and eventually to Italy.

chance: a style of composition in which decisions normally made by composers were left to the performers in the moment of performance.

chanson: a secular song with French words; used primarily in the fourteenth to sixteenth centuries to describe French polyphonic songs.

characteristic music: music that suggests a mood, personality, or scene that is usually suggested by the title.

choral society: local amateur choruses that first began appearing in the nineteenth century.

chorale prelude: a short musical setting of a chorale melody to be played on the organ before or during the congregational singing of a hymn.

chorale: a strophic, congregational hymn in the Lutheran tradition.

clavichord: a Baroque period keyboard instrument who strings are struck by tangents that remain in contact until the key is released.

concertato medium: the seventeenth-century development in which voices and instruments would play parts independent of each other.

concerted madrigal: type of madrigal in the early seventeenth century in which one or more voices were accompanied by basso continuo.

concertino: a small ensemble of instrumental soloists that play in contrast to the full orchestra in a concerto.

concerto grosso: an instrumental composition in which a small solo ensemble is juxtaposed against the full orchestra.

concerto: a term that changes in meaning over time, it generally refers compositions for instrumental ensembles.

conductor: a person who leads a performance for orchestra, band, or chorus by means of gestures.

continuo group: the group of keyboard, bass stringed instruments, and strummed instruments that played the bass line in Baroque music.

contrafactum: the process of adding new words to an existing song or melody.

court ballet: a seventeenth-century French musical-dramatic work of multiple movements that was a prominent feature of the court of King Louis XIV.

development: the second part of the sonata form in which musical material from the exposition is reworked in new ways and combinations while wandering through a variety of keys.

doctrine of affections: the belief that human emotions were states of being in the soul, and each one was caused by spirits in the body.

empfindsam style: a term originating in the Classical period marked by surprising turns in harmony, anxious rhythmic activity, and free, speech-like melodies.

episode: a subsidiary passage between presentations of the main thematic material.

equal temperament: a system of tuning used in Western music today in which the octave is divided into twelve equal semitones; the octave is the only perfectly tuned interval.

étude: a composition for piano intended serve as a pedagogical tool in piano studies.

experimental music: a twentieth-century trend in music that focused on exploring new sounds, techniques, and resources.

exposition: the first part of the sonata form in which two different themes or theme groups are presented.

fantasia: an instrumental composition that mimics improvisation and is free in form.

First Viennese School: refers collectively to eighteenth-century composers Wolfgang Amadeus Mozart, Joseph Haydn, and Ludwig van Beethoven.

formes fixes: fourteenth-century song forms that prescribed a particular pattern of repetition for text and music.

French overture: the principal instrumental music used to open an opera or ballet, marked by two distinct, contrasting, repeated sections.

frottola: sixteenth-century Italian strophic song, in which the text was set mostly syllabically with the melody in the uppermost voice.

fugue: a compositional form that employs a strict method of imitation; it was established firmly in the Baroque period.

galant: a descriptor of the classic style; a French term that came to encompass anything that was modern, chic, sophisticated, and in style.

ground bass: see basso ostinato.

historia: a musical composition based on a biblical story

homophony: a musical texture where all voices move together at the same time, as distinct from polyphony.

humanism: a revival of ancient thought, philosophy, and learning inspired by a renewed interest in classical Latin and Greek writings.

idée fixe: a term coined by Hector Berlioz for a melodic theme that is used throughout a composition to represent a person, thing, or idea and is transformed to suit the mood and situation.

imitation mass: a polyphonic mass that borrows all of the voices from an existing polyphonic work, such as a motet or chanson.

indeterminacy: a style of composition in which the composer leaves certain aspects of the music unspecified.

intabulation: a published manuscript of vocal arrangements for keyboardists and lutists.

just intonation: a system of tuning voices from the Renaissance in which most thirds, sixths, fourths, and fifths are perfectly in tune.

leitmotive: a German term in opera or music drama in which a motive, theme, or musical idea associated with a person, situation, thing, mood, or idea returns frequently in original or altered form.

lied: the German word for "song," it refers to German art songs developed in the Romantic period.

liturgy: the body of texts to be spoken or sung and ritual actions to be performed in a religious service.

lute song: sixteenth-century English solo song with lute accompaniment.

madrigal: a form of secular polyphonic music; the meaning of the term changes over time.

masque: an English form of court entertainment that was similar to the French court ballet.

Mass Ordinary: refers to the portions of the Mass that were the same at every celebration.

Mass Proper: refers to all texts in the Mass that change according to the church calendar, and thus were different at every Mass.

melismatic chant: chant that features long melodic passages set to a single syllable of text.

mensuration signs: fourteenth-century symbols placed at the beginning of music to indicate the rhythmic and metric profile of the music; the ancestors of today's modern time signatures.

metrical psalm: rhymed, metered, strophic psalms of the Calvinist church that have been translated into the vernacular and set to new melodies or existing chant tunes.

minimalism: a compositional technique in which all musical materials (e.g. rhythms and pitches) are kept to an absolute minimum and simplified, so that the music itself is transparent and obvious.

modal music: music based on a series of notes who have a particular intervallic relationship; common of the Middle Ages and Renaissance.

modernism: twentieth-century musical movement in which composers sought a radical break from the musical language of their predecessors while maintaining some strong ties to tradition.

modified strophic form: a song form in which music is repeated for some stanzas of the poetry, but is changed or uses new music for others.

motet: a polyphonic vocal composition, whose specific meaning changes over time.

motto mass: polyphonic mass in which a single melody is used as the beginning pitches in one or all voices.

music drama: nineteenth-century genre developed by Richard Wagner in which music and drama are organically connected in a collective artwork.

musica universalis: also known as "music of the spheres," it is a theory that the planets, sun, and moon all produce a sound or hum based on their orbits, having an effect on the inhabitants of earth.

neoclassicism: a musical trend in the first half of the twentieth-century in which composers sought to revive, imitate, and evoke the styles, genres, and forms of pre-Romantic music.

neo-Romanticism: a twentieth-century trend in which composers adopted the familiar musical language and expressivity of nineteenth-century Romantic music.

neumatic chant: chant where each syllable of text is set to one to six pitches.

neumes: small signs in early chant notation that indicated the number of pitches per syllable and the ascent or descent of the melody.

New German School: refers collectively to nineteenth-century composers Richard Wagner, Hector Berlioz, and Franz Liszt.

nocturne: a character piece for solo piano popularized by Chopin in which beautiful melodies soar above rich harmonies.

oratorio: a genre of dramatic religious music that combines elements of narrative, dialogue, and commentary.

orchestra: an instrumental ensemble whose core is stringed instruments with multiple players on each part.

orchestral concerto: an instrumental composition of the Baroque that focused on the contrast between the first violin part and the bass.

organum: a medieval form of polyphony where one or more voices are added to an existing line of chant.

paraphrase mass: a polyphonic mass in which each movement is based on the same existing melody, which is paraphrased in all voices.

partbook: a manuscript or printed book that contained the music for a single voice or instrument, with a complete set needed to perform a musical work.

partsong: nineteenth-century form of choral music that was similar to the Lied.

passion: a type of historia that recalls the suffering and death of Jesus' crucifixion

polyphony: a method of music composition in which voices sing together on completely independent parts.

polystylism: a twentieth-century term for music that combines new and old musical styles through either direct quotation or allusion.

prepared piano: an invention by John Cage in which various objects are inserted between the strings of a piano, creating new, complex percussive sounds when played from the keyboard.

prima prattica: a term used in the seventeenth century meaning "first practice;" refers to the sixteenth-century style of polyphony.

primitivism: a twentieth-century style that characterizes the early music of Stravinsky, which is marked by insistent dissonance, heavy percussiveness, and pounding rhythms.

programmatic music: a composition that specifically recounts a particular narrative or tale, often delineated in an accompanying text called a program.

Pythagorean tuning: a system of tuning voices from the Middle Ages in which all intervals of a perfect fourth and fifth are perfectly in tune.

recapitulation: the third and final part of the sonata in which the musical material from the exposition returns and brings the movement to a close.

recitative: musical, free, speech-like declamations of text

requiem: the Roman Catholic rite of a funeral mass; also known as the Latin Mass for the Dead.

ricercare: an instrumental composition that treats one or more musical subjects or themes imitatively

ritornello form: a Baroque form of composition, typically in concertos, in which a refrain played by the full orchestra alternates with episodes played by the soloist(s).

ritornello: Italian for "refrain;" generally refers to any section of music that is presented and then returns over the course of a piece; the term varies in meaning over time.

sacred concerto: a seventeenth-century genre that adopted a theatrical element in the setting of religious texts, accompanying them by basso continuo and incorporating elements of the concertato medium and operatic styles.

Second Viennese School: refers collectively to twentieth-century composers Arnold Schoenberg, Alban Berg, and Anton Webern.

seconda prattica: a term used in the seventeenth century meaning "second practice," refers to a new style of breaking established rules of composition, introducing more dissonance into music, and seeking to more convincingly convey the feelings and meaning of the text.

serial music: music that applies the twelve-tone method of composition, especially music that uses the same approach in musical elements other than pitch.

sinfonia: a generic term applied in the seventeenth century to any abstract instrumental composition.

solo concerto: an instrumental composition which a single soloist is juxtaposed against the full orchestra.

sonata form: a three-part form typical of the Classical and Romantic periods, most commonly found in the first movements of sonatas, chamber works, and symphonies.

sonata: generally a composition to be played by one or more instruments, often in multiple movements; the term changes over time.

song cycle: a collection of songs that are meant to be performed consecutively like a multimovement work.

sprechstimme: a twentieth-century compositional technique in which a singer approximates written pitches in a gliding, speech-like tone while following the rhythm exactly.

stile antico: style used in music written after 1600 that imitated the old style of Palestrina, particularly for church music.

stile concitato: a reference to the "excited style" of the seventeenth and eighteenth centuries.

stile moderno: seventeenth-century style of compositions that used basso continuo and applied the rules of the seconda prattica.

string quartet: standard chamber ensemble consisting of two violins, one viola, and one cello; also the term for a multimovement work composed for such an ensemble.

suite: a set of pieces combined into a single work; in the Baroque it consisted of a set of stylized dance pieces.

syllabic chant: chant where each syllable of text is set to only one pitch.

symphonic poem: a nineteenth-century one-movement programmatic work that was suggested by a picture, play, poem, or other art form.

symphony: a multimovement orchestral composition in which all members of the ensemble play together without a separation between soloist and orchestra.

text depiction: the use of musical gestures to suggest or reinforce an image.

text expression: conveying the meaning or emotions in a text through musical means.

toccata: a genre of keyboard music that either is or sounds improvisatory in nature.

tonal music: music based on the seventeenth-century system in which music is organized around an emphasis note or chord, to which all others are subordinate.

total serialism: the methodological application of serialism to all musical elements in a composition.

trecento: refers to the music of Italy in the 1300s.

variation: the process of reworking a given melody, theme, song and the varied forms that result from it; may be either compositional or improvisatory.

villancico: a short, strophic Spanish song usually on a rustic or popular topic.

About the Author

R. Ryan Endris, D. Mus, currently serves as Assistant Professor of Music and Director of Choral Activities at Colgate University. He is also in demand as an arranger of choral and instrumental music throughout the country, and his arrangements have been heard by audiences around the world. Dr. Endris holds Doctor of Music and Master of Music of Choral Conducting degrees from the Indiana University Jacobs School of Music, as well as a Bachelor of Music Education (K-12 Choral/General Music). He has studied voice with internationally acclaimed soprano Sylvia McNair, and his conducting teachers and mentors include Robert Porco of the Cleveland Orchestra; John Poole of the BBC Singers; Dale Warland of the Dale Warland Singers; and Vance George, Director Emeritus of the San Francisco Symphony Chorus.

About the Artist

Joe Lee is an illustrator, cartoonist, writer, and clown. With a degree from Indiana University centering on Medieval History, Joe is also a graduate of Ringling Brothers, Barnum and Bailey's Clown College. He worked for some years as a circus clown. He is the illustrator of a several For Beginners books, his most recent being *Greek Mythology For Beginners*. Joe lives in Bloomington, Indiana with his wife Mary Bess, son Brandon, cat George, and the terriers (or rather terrors) Max and Jack.

THE FOR BEGINNERS® SERIES

AFRICAN HISTORY FOR BEGINNERS   ISBN 978-1-934389-18-€

ANARCHISM FOR BEGINNERS   ISBN 978-1-934389-32-4

ARABS & ISRAEL FOR BEGINNERS   ISBN 978-1-934389-16-4

ART THEORY FOR BEGINNERS   ISBN 978-1-934389-47-8

ASTRONOMY FOR BEGINNERS   ISBN 978-1-934389-25-6

AYN RAND FOR BEGINNERS   ISBN 978-1-934389-37-9

BARACK OBAMA FOR BEGINNERS, AN ESSENTIAL GUIDE   ISBN 978-1-934389-44-7

BEN FRANKLIN FOR BEGINNERS   ISBN 978-1-934389-48-5

BLACK HISTORY FOR BEGINNERS   ISBN 978-1-934389-19-5

THE BLACK HOLOCAUST FOR BEGINNERS   ISBN 978-1-934389-03-4

BLACK WOMEN FOR BEGINNERS   ISBN 978-1-934389-20-1

CHOMSKY FOR BEGINNERS   ISBN 978-1-934389-17-1

DADA & SURREALISM FOR BEGINNERS   ISBN 978-1-934389-00-3

DANTE FOR BEGINNERS   ISBN 978-1-934389-67-6

DECONSTRUCTION FOR BEGINNERS   ISBN 978-1-934389-26-3

DEMOCRACY FOR BEGINNERS   ISBN 978-1-934389-36-2

DERRIDA FOR BEGINNERS   ISBN 978-1-934389-11-9

EASTERN PHILOSOPHY FOR BEGINNERS   ISBN 978-1-934389-07-2

EXISTENTIALISM FOR BEGINNERS   ISBN 978-1-934389-21-8

FANON FOR BEGINNERS   ISBN 978-1-934389-87-4

FDR AND THE NEW DEAL FOR BEGINNERS   ISBN 978-1-934389-50-8

FOUCAULT FOR BEGINNERS   ISBN 978-1-934389-12-6

GENDER & SEXUALITY FOR BEGINNERS   ISBN 978-1-934389-69-0

GLOBAL WARMING FOR BEGINNERS   ISBN 978-1-934389-27-0

GREEK MYTHOLOGY FOR BEGINNERS   ISBN 978-1-934389-83-6

HEIDEGGER FOR BEGINNERS   ISBN 978-1-934389-13-3

THE HISTORY OF CLASSICAL MUSIC FOR BEGINNERS   ISBN 978-1-939994-26-4

THE HISTORY OF OPERA FOR BEGINNERS   ISBN 978-1-934389-79-9

ISLAM FOR BEGINNERS   ISBN 978-1-934389-01-0

JANE AUSTEN FOR BEGINNERS   ISBN 978-1-934389-61-4

JUNG FOR BEGINNERS   ISBN 978-1-934389-76-8

KIERKEGAARD FOR BEGINNERS   ISBN 978-1-934389-14-0

LACAN FOR BEGINNERS   ISBN 978-1-934389-39-3

LINGUISTICS FOR BEGINNERS   ISBN 978-1-934389-28-7

MALCOLM X FOR BEGINNERS   ISBN 978-1-934389-04-1

MARX'S DAS KAPITAL FOR BEGINNERS   ISBN 978-1-934389-59-1

MCLUHAN FOR BEGINNERS   ISBN 978-1-934389-75-1

NIETZSCHE FOR BEGINNERS   ISBN 978-1-934389-05-8

PAUL ROBESON FOR BEGINNERS   ISBN 978-1-934389-81-2

PHILOSOPHY FOR BEGINNERS   ISBN 978-1-934389-02-7

PLATO FOR BEGINNERS   ISBN 978-1-934389-08-9

POETRY FOR BEGINNERS   ISBN 978-1-934389-46-1

POSTMODERNISM FOR BEGINNERS   ISBN 978-1-934389-09-6

RELATIVITY & QUANTUM PHYSICS FOR BEGINNERS   ISBN 978-1-934389-42-3

SARTRE FOR BEGINNERS   ISBN 978-1-934389-15-7

SHAKESPEARE FOR BEGINNERS   ISBN 978-1-934389-29-4

STRUCTURALISM & POSTSTRUCTURALISM FOR BEGINNERS   ISBN 978-1-934389-10-2

WOMEN'S HISTORY FOR BEGINNERS   ISBN 978-1-934389-60-7

UNIONS FOR BEGINNERS   ISBN 978-1-934389-77-5

U.S. CONSTITUTION FOR BEGINNERS   ISBN 978-1-934389-62-1

ZEN FOR BEGINNERS   ISBN 978-1-934389-06-5

ZINN FOR BEGINNERS   ISBN 978-1-934389-40-9